S·H·P

THE
SCHOOLS
HISTORY
PROJECT

DISCOVERING THE PAST

THE CHANGING ROLE OF WOMEN

Liz Bellamy
Kate Moorse
Colin Shephard (series editor)

JOHN MURRAY

THE SCHOOLS HISTORY PROJECT

This project was set up by the Schools Council in 1972. Its main aim was to suggest suitable objectives for history teachers, and to promote the use of appropriate materials and teaching methods for their realization. This involved a reconsideration of the nature of history and its relevance in secondary schools, the design of a syllabus framework that shows the uses of history in the teaching of adolescents, and the setting up of appropriate examinations.

Since 1978 the project has been based at Trinity and All Saints' College, Leeds. It is now self-funding and with the advent of the National Curriculum it has expanded its publications to provide courses throughout Key Stages 1–3, and for a range of GCSE and A level syllabuses. The project provides INSET for all aspects of National Curriculum, GCSE and A level history, and also publishes *Discoveries*, a twice-yearly journal for history teachers.

Enquiries about the project, INSET and *Discoveries* should be addressed to the Schools History Project, Trinity and All Saints' College, Brownberrie Lane, Horsforth, Leeds LS18 5HD.

Enquiries about the *Discovering the Past* series should be addressed to the publishers, John Murray.

Series consultants

Terry Fiehn
Tim Lomas
Martin and Jenny Tucker

© Liz Bellamy, Kate Moorse 1996

First published in 1996
by John Murray (Publishers) Ltd
50 Albemarle Street, London W1X 4BD

Layouts by Ann Samuel
Typeset by Wearset, Boldon, Tyne and Wear
Printed in Great Britain by the University Press, Cambridge

A CIP record for this book is available from the British Library
ISBN 0–7195–5106–4

Contents

The changing role of women

As YOU work through this book, you will find out how the role of women has changed over the past 1,000 years, from the Middle Ages until the twentieth century.

▲SOURCE 1

▲SOURCE 2

◀ SOURCE 3

WE WANT THE VOTE TO STOP THE WHITE SLAVE TRAFFIC, SWEATED LABOUR, AND TO SAVE THE CHILDREN.

THE APPEAL OF WOMANHOOD

▲SOURCE 4

▲SOURCE 5

▲SOURCE 6

▲SOURCE 7

▼SOURCE 8

1. Study Sources 1–8 carefully. Put them in the correct chronological order. You can ask your teacher for a timeline to help you.
2. Choose two sources that suggest that women's lives changed a lot during the period, and two sources that suggest that they did not. Explain your choice.

How do we find out about medieval women?

THE FIRST period you are going to study in detail is the Middle Ages. On these two pages there are descriptions of six women who lived in the Middle Ages. The pictures have been drawn by a modern artist, who had to imagine what the women looked like, but the women were all real people, and the descriptions of them are based on written evidence from the Middle Ages.

Alice Coleman, wife of Ricard Coleman, lived in Brigstock in Northamptonshire. She looked after her home and family, but was also an 'ale-wife', which means she brewed and sold ale (another name for beer). Ale was drunk by everyone, because water was often unhealthy. It was a high-energy drink (full of starch and sugar) and so was an important part of people's diet, which was otherwise mainly bread and soup. The ale-wife was a well-known figure in the medieval village or town. Alice Coleman sold ale between 1299 and 1325. According to the manorial court records, when she finally gave up the business it was taken over by her daughter.

Juliana Wheeler was a money-lender working in Hagley, Worcestershire, in the late fourteenth century. We know about her through the records of the manorial courts, as in 1387 she took Philip Brough to court to make him repay a loan of three marks.

Emma Northcote was a single woman from a poor background. She worked as a servant in the household of Philip Seys, an important man in local politics in Exeter. She also worked as a prostitute. Most of her clients were priests, including John Gonlok, who kept up a relationship with her for over four years. She had trouble getting payment for her services on some occasions. We know this because the manorial court records show that she took at least nine men to court, including three priests, for payment of money owed to her.

Emma Taillor was also known as Emma Hosiere. She made stockings for a living in medieval Exeter. She had her own business, rather than working for someone else, and she was registered as the head of her household in the tax return of 1387. This was a fairly unusual position for a woman at this time. The fact that she paid tax of twelve pence suggests that she was quite a rich and successful businesswoman.

4

Like many medieval women, **Matilda Monioun** (below left) had a number of occupations. She brewed and sold ale over a period of sixteen years, and also sold butter, eggs, cheese and sometimes fish, as well as making woollen cloth. Her activities were not always strictly legal; on several occasions she was accused of receiving stolen wool, thread and other goods.

1. Get a copy of this chart from your teacher. Use the descriptions of the six women to fill out as much of it as you can.

Name of woman			
When she lived			
Where she lived			
What job she did			
What else you know about her			
How we know about her			

2. We know about four of these women because they appeared at the manorial courts. Why did they appear before the manorial courts?
3. How might historians have found out about the other two women?
4. Write four sentences summing up the kinds of lives these women lived.
5. As a class, discuss whether you think these six medieval women are typical of all medieval women.

Katherine Ruthven (above right) was married to Sir Colin Campbell of Glenorchy in Scotland. The family records, which survive to this day, show that the Campbell family was wealthy. They describe the tasks Katherine had to do to organise a busy household. She also did a tremendous amount of sewing and embroidery. After her marriage in 1550 she set about creating a whole series of bed covers, wall hangings and cushions. One survives – you can see it in Source 1.

SOURCE 1 A tapestry by Katherine Ruthven. It shows Adam and Eve in the garden of Eden and is based on a popular picture of the time

HOW DO WE FIND OUT ABOUT MEDIEVAL WOMEN?

When we try to find out about medieval women, we discover that most of the evidence is about women like those on the previous page. They are:

- women from wealthy families who kept household accounts, *or*
- women who ran their own businesses and had to pay tax, *or*
- women who ran the sort of business that was controlled by the manorial court, *or*
- women who went to court to make someone pay money owed to them, *or*
- women who were taken to court for a crime they had committed.

We know about these women because written evidence such as household records, tax returns or manorial court records have survived. But these women are not really typical of medieval women.

- Most women were poor not rich.
- Most women did not have their own businesses. According to a 1319 tax return for London, only four per cent of taxpayers in London were women.
- Most women never went to the manorial courts.

The information we have about the role of these more ordinary women is sketchy and vague. Historians studying the history of women find that they tend not to appear in **the main sources**. This is because they were not usually involved in the activities that were most likely to be recorded. Even in recent periods women's lives have not been recorded in the same detail as men's lives. Throughout this unit, therefore, you are going to be faced with the problem of lack of evidence.

For this reason, finding out about the changing role of women requires skill and subtlety. We have to find out what we can from the sources, and then fill in the gaps in our knowledge. We must also be prepared to revise our first conclusions when we discover new evidence, because every individual we find out about can tell us something more about medieval society as a whole.

Margery, the widow of William

Source 3 is from a survey of the village of Ardleigh in Hertfordshire. It includes details of one woman, Margery, who was living in the village in 1222. What can this simple entry tell us about her, or how she lived?

The source gives us only a little information. Apart from this, we can only make guesses based on what we know about other medieval women. Perhaps Margery has grown-up sons who help her out; some women did. Or then again, perhaps she has never had children.

She may have taken up her husband's trade, although female blacksmiths were unusual. If she has become a blacksmith, she may be sharing the profits with a male assistant.

Like most medieval women, she probably does some spinning of wool to make a little extra money.

What other talents does she have? She may be a great singer or cook, or a wonderful mother. She may be breathtakingly beautiful, or an awe-inspiring figure. We simply do not know. If we searched hard we might be lucky and find out more about her from manorial records. But she will only appear there if she takes part in an activity that is controlled by the courts – that is, if she buys or sells land, if she bakes bread or brews beer, or if she does something wrong and is taken to court. If, like most women, Margery lives an ordinary, undistinguished life, we are never likely to find out about any extraordinary qualities she may have possessed.

SOURCE 2 A modern cartoonist's view of the way that women have appeared in history books

SOURCE 3 A survey of landholding in the parish of Ardleigh in 1222 gives the following information

> *These [people] hold land from the lord of the manor:*
> *Ralph son of William of Crawnie 3 acres for 12d.*
> *Roger son of Ailwinus 6 acres for 2s.*
> *Geoffrey son of John 7 acres for 2s. and 4d.*
> *   Also 8 acres for 32d.*
> *Odo son of William 8 acres for 32d.*
> *William son of Godwin 3 acres for 12d.*
> *Michael son of Adam 1 acre for 2d., which Nicholas the Canon gave to him.*
> *William Abel half an acre for 2d. with the daughter of Blidewinus.*
> *Margery the widow of William the smith 3 roods for 6d.*

We don't know how old she is, but she is a widow – i.e. her husband has died, and she has not remarried since his death.

Margery's husband was a blacksmith. A blacksmith was a skilled craftsman, and the job was quite an important one in village life. A blacksmith had to make and mend farm tools and household equipment. He also had to shoe horses.

The portion of land she rents from the lord of the manor is the smallest in the village. A rood is about 30 metres square. This is not enough for her to grow enough food to live on. We do not know how else she supports herself.

SOURCE 4 A medieval peasant shearing a sheep

SOURCE 6 A blacksmith's workshop in the Middle Ages

SOURCE 7 A woman milking a cow

SOURCE 5 A medieval peasant's cottage

1. Look at Sources 4–7. Each of these pictures can help us fill in the gaps in Margery's life. For each one, explain what aspect of Margery's life the source might help us find out about.
2. Use Sources 4–7 to help you write a paragraph to describe what you think life was like for Margery.

Activity

On a large piece of paper write out a list of questions you would like to ask about the lives of women in the Middle Ages.

In one colour circle the questions which you think it will be easiest to answer. In another colour circle the ones it will be most difficult to answer.

What did medieval women do?

MOST women in the Middle Ages seem to have done a number of different sorts of work:

■ They made and sold certain types of goods.

■ They looked after the house, the garden and any farm animals.

■ They had and cared for children.

■ They helped out their fathers or husbands in their businesses.

■ In the countryside, they worked on the family's land when extra labour was required.

Sources 1–10 show or describe women's occupations in the Middle Ages. They all come from fourteenth- or fifteenth-century manuscripts. Many of the pictures show scenes from Italy, France or Belgium, because there are very few pictures of everyday English life in this period. But they show activities which would have happened in England.

> **SOURCE 1** From a survey of a village in Leicestershire in the fifteenth century
>
> *Women were recorded doing the following jobs:*
> - *haymaking*
> - *weeding*
> - *mowing*
> - *carrying corn*
> - *breaking stones for road-mending*
> - *working as thatchers' labourers.*

> **SOURCE 2** The following women are listed in a London tax return of 1319. Can you work out what each of them did for a living?
>
> *Petronilla le Brewere*
> *Margeria la Sylkewymman*
> *Alic la Stocfysshmonger*
> *Dyonisia la Bokebyndere*
> *E. Scolemaysteresse*

SOURCE 3

1. Make a list of all the jobs shown or mentioned in the sources.
2. Choose two different pictures to look at in detail. Work out:
   a) whether each job is being done indoors or outdoors.
   b) whether you think it is easy or hard work.
   c) what equipment is needed for it.
   d) whether women are doing the job alone or with others.
3. Which of these words best describe the women's work shown in these sources: hard, varied, easy, interesting, difficult, lonely, boring? Explain your choice.
4. Which of the jobs shown in the sources would you have preferred?

SOURCE 4

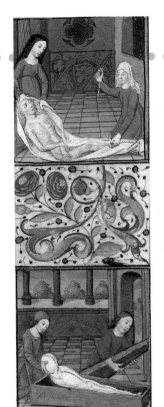

▲ SOURCE 5

▲ SOURCE 7

◄ SOURCE 8

▼ SOURCE 9

▲SOURCE 6

▼ SOURCE 10

WHAT DID MEDIEVAL WOMEN DO?

How were women workers treated?

Many jobs in the Middle Ages were done by both men and women. But did this mean that they were treated equally? Source 11 is a chart from the Middle Ages showing what men and women were supposed to be paid per day for various farming jobs.

SOURCE 11

	With meat and drink	Without meat and drink
The man Reaper	8 pence	14 pence
The woman Reaper	5 pence	9 pence
Hay maker the man	6 pence	12 pence
Hay maker the woman	4 pence	8 pence
Women and such impotent persons that weed corn and other such like Labourers	2 pence	6 pence
The man Clipper of Sheep	7 pence	14 pence
The woman Clipper of Sheep	6 pence	12 pence

1. Read Source 11. Which are the best-paid and worst-paid jobs?
2. What reasons can you think of to explain the differences in pay between the men and women?
3. What reasons can you think of to explain the differences in pay between the different types of work?

In towns and cities working life was much more strictly controlled than in the countryside. The crafts and trades organised themselves into GUILDS and made rules about who could carry out a trade. In this way, men often prevented women from doing certain types of work. For example, a Memorandum Book from York lists the following jobs that were open to women in the 1400s: cap-maker, glover, parchment-maker, dyer, barber-surgeon, bow-stringer, tanner. They were not allowed to carry out other crafts and trades.

In other cities women were allowed to enter certain trades only if they had a father or a husband in the business. However, there is evidence from the Middle Ages that even this was sometimes forbidden, as you can see in Source 12.

SOURCE 12 From weavers' records of 1461

Various people of the weavers' craft in the said town of Bristol employ their wives, daughters and maids either to weave at their own looms, or to work for someone else at the same craft. As a result many men, learned in the craft of weaving, are unemployed and cannot earn a living. From this day forth, no weaver may employ his wife, daughter or maid in the occupation of weaving at a loom, and anyone doing so will be fined 6 shillings and 8 pence.

Many men and women worked as servants in the homes of rich people. Servants were under the control of their masters or mistresses. Source 13 shows how mistresses were told to treat women who worked for them as maidservants.

SOURCE 13 From a thirteenth-century book, *On the Properties of Things*, by Bartholomew the Englishman

A handmaid is to obey the wife. She must do the harder and lower duties. She feeds on the coarser food, wears the rougher clothing . . . she may not marry according to her wishes.

Fear keeps servants and handmaids in their place. Kindly affection sometimes makes them arrogant.

SOURCE 14 A mistress beating her maidservant, from a fourteenth-century manuscript

4. Does the impression of women's jobs given by Sources 11–14 support or conflict with the impression given by Sources 1–10? Explain your answer.

Town and country, rich and poor

Two of the most important factors that determined what work women did were:

■ whether they lived in a town or in the country
■ whether they were rich or poor.

In the later Middle Ages the vast majority of women (ninety per cent) lived in the countryside. Only ten per cent lived in the towns or cities.

Of the ten per cent who lived in towns or cities, most of them – about eighty per cent – were poor. Only twenty per cent were rich. They were mainly the wives and daughters of merchants and skilled craftsmen. Source 15 shows you the kinds of work each group did.

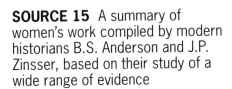

SOURCE 15 A summary of women's work compiled by modern historians B.S. Anderson and J.P. Zinsser, based on their study of a wide range of evidence

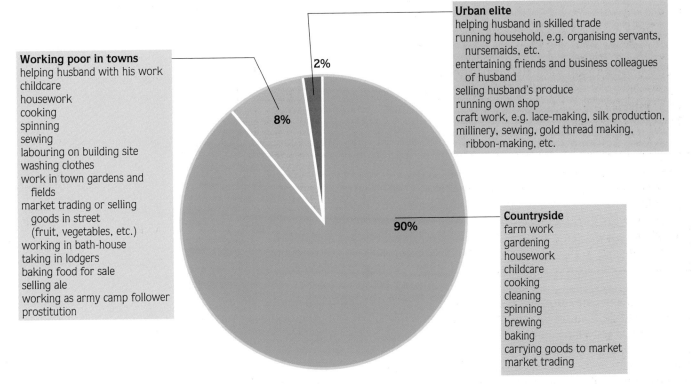

Working poor in towns
helping husband with his work
childcare
housework
cooking
spinning
sewing
labouring on building site
washing clothes
work in town gardens and
    fields
market trading or selling
    goods in street
    (fruit, vegetables, etc.)
working in bath-house
taking in lodgers
baking food for sale
selling ale
working as army camp follower
prostitution

Urban elite
helping husband in skilled trade
running household, e.g. organising servants,
    nursemaids, etc.
entertaining friends and business colleagues
    of husband
selling husband's produce
running own shop
craft work, e.g. lace-making, silk production,
millinery, sewing, gold thread making,
    ribbon-making, etc.

Countryside
farm work
gardening
housework
childcare
cooking
cleaning
spinning
brewing
baking
carrying goods to market
market trading

2%

8%

90%

1. Look at all the women shown or described on the last eight pages. For each woman, write down whether she was: urban rich; urban poor; countryside.
2. Make a list of all the kinds of evidence about women used on pages 6–11.
3. What kinds of evidence have we not used which you think we might be able to use?
4. Write your own essay on 'What kinds of work did women do in the Middle Ages?' Your teacher can give you an outline to help you.

Life cycles

THROUGHOUT the Middle Ages there were limits on what women could do.

Legal rules

Women could not:
- marry without their parents' consent
- inherit land from their parents, unless they had no surviving brothers
- own property of any kind – even clothes or jewellery – unless they were widows
- own their own business without special permission
- have custody of their children
- divorce their husbands.

Career rules

Women could not:
- go to university
- train to be a doctor or lawyer
- become a priest
- join the army or navy
- become a judge
- become a Member of Parliament.

Rules of good behaviour

These applied mostly to rich women. For poor peasants and servants, who had to work, they were less rigid. Some of these restrictions affected young women more than older women. Women could not:
- go to shops, inns and taverns on their own
- go on journeys by themselves
- spend time alone with a man
- wear tight or revealing clothes or use make-up
- speak rudely
- read books their parents did not approve of.

You are now going to look at two women's lives in detail, to see how a woman's life varied from childhood through to old age.

As you find out about their lives, think about how they are similar to or different from the lives of women today.

Childhood

Children were completely under the control of their parents. However, what life was like for girls varied according to how rich their families were.

Claude de France was a princess, born in 1499. She was French, but her life was very much like the life of a rich English girl.

As a child, she had servants to look after her and feed her. She did not see much of her parents. She probably played games such as those shown in Sources 2 and 3.

She also had a teacher who taught her to read and told her Bible stories from a 'primer'. Source 4 shows a page from Claude's primer.

When she was only five Claude's father arranged whom she should marry: her cousin Francis, who was a prince. From then on, the main purpose of her education was to teach her the correct behaviour for a noblewoman. Source 1 shows the kind of things she would be taught.

Claude was taught to read the Bible and her prayer book for herself. There was not much else to read, as printing had only just been invented.

Claude was also taught how to sew and embroider. She was probably taught to play a musical instrument – most rich girls were. She would also learn how to dress, how to talk correctly, and even how to look at other people.

She would not have had boyfriends, and when she met her future husband, Francis, a woman called a chaperone would have stayed to watch over them.

SOURCE 1 The French *Book of the Knight of La Tour Landry*, which was translated into English in 1484, gave advice to upper-class parents on how to bring up their daughters. These are the things it said a girl should learn:

> *Be humble and polite to rich and poor; keep her body pure and clean; be humble, polite and useful to her husband; and learn to read.*

SOURCE 2
Children playing frog-in-the-middle

SOURCE 3 A young child with a baby walker

Compare Claude with **Martha**, a peasant girl. Martha was mentioned in manorial records from the fourteenth century as milking sheep in the small village of Elton. However, those records do not even give her a name, so we have called her Martha. There is no other record of her life, so we have had to collect together evidence from other sources to build up a picture of what her life might have been like.

Like Claude, Martha was under the control of her parents. Unlike Claude, she was expected to help her mother with housework from a very early age. She would have learned the traditional female jobs: looking after the animals, spinning, cooking, brewing, cheese-making and looking after younger children.

She still had time to play. In fact, some of her games might have been very similar to Claude's. But from the age of ten most of her life would have been spent working.

SOURCE 4 Girls were taught to read from a 'primer'. This had simple prayers and Bible stories in it, as well as an alphabet. This is the front page of Claude's primer. She is shown wearing a brown dress and holding a closed book

SOURCE 5 A peasant child helps her mother with the cooking, from a medieval manuscript

1. Use the evidence on these two pages to complete a chart like this, showing how Claude and Martha's lives were similar to/different from your life.

	Claude	Martha
similarities to your life		
differences from your life		

LIFE CYCLES

Getting married

Nowadays teenagers are not thought of as children, but are not yet considered to be adults. For medieval women it was rather different. Once they were over the age of ten or eleven they were treated as adults.

Girls like Claude, from richer families, would be married while they were still in their early teens. Girls like Martha, from poor families, would be working almost full time by the time they were ten years old, and would carry on in much the same way until they were married.

Marriage marked the beginning of the next phase of their life cycle, although for Claude and Martha it would have happened at different ages.

Claude de France married her cousin Francis when she was just fourteen. The marriage was arranged by her father. This was not unusual for a child of a rich family.

Her parents' aim in arranging the marriage was to strengthen the links between two rich and powerful families. It was not important whether Claude loved Francis.

Arranging a marriage for a rich girl usually involved a DOWRY – that is, the parents of the bride gave money or property to the parents of the groom.

Marriage for poorer girls, such as Martha, might also have been arranged by their parents. Martha's parents would certainly have needed to agree to her marriage, because until she got married they still controlled everything she did.

Most marriages were between people from the same class. A peasant woman, such as Martha, would usually marry a peasant man. The daughter of a craftsman would often marry the son of a craftsman.

Like Claude's, Martha's marriage would have involved handing over some money or property to the groom's family as a dowry.

Early in the Middle Ages people did not go to church to get married. It was late in the Middle Ages that marriage became a church ceremony. Even then, many poor people disliked a church wedding because it was expensive. Instead the priest married them at the church door, or elsewhere in the village.

Poor women married at a later age than rich women. A peasant girl, such as Martha, would have been unlikely to marry before she was in her mid to late twenties.

◀ **SOURCE 6** A medieval wedding

---

1. Look at Source 6. Do you think this shows the wedding of a rich woman or a poor woman? Explain your answer.
2. Why do you think a girl's parents were expected to pay a dowry?

Married life

Once a woman was married, her role in society changed considerably. She was free of her parents' control, but instead she came under the control of her husband. She still had no legal rights, but on the other hand she did have the responsibility of running her own household, which needed a range of different skills.

Sources 7 and 8 show what was expected of the ideal wife in two different classes.

Source 7 describes the kind of life **Claude de France** would have lived. It was written by a wealthy fourteenth-century businessman, the Menagier de Paris. The book contains all kinds of information on household management, from recipes and remedies to tips on handling domestic servants. This is his description of how a young wife should spend her time.

Source 8 was written by Sir Anthony Fitzherbert in the sixteenth century. He was a member of the upper classes, but his *Book of Husbandry* was intended to show small farmers (and their wives) how they should go about their business.

1. Compare Sources 7 and 8. Find two similarities and two differences between the life of the rich woman and the life of the farmer's wife.
2. Source 7 was written 200 years before Source 8, and is about a wife from a different social class. Which of these two factors best explains the differences between the lives of the two women?
3. From all that you have found out about the Middle Ages, how do you think the life of a peasant woman such as Martha would have been different from that of the farmer's wife in Source 8? Explain your answer.

SOURCE 7 A day in the life of a medieval gentlewoman

It is not fitting for a wealthy married woman to get up at dawn, for that is when nuns and servants get up. After rising, a gentlewoman should wash her face and hands, say her prayers, get dressed, and go to Mass. On her return to the house, she should check that the servants have done their work properly, and speak to the steward about the arrangements for dinner and supper. If she is in her country house, she should ensure that the farm animals have been looked after. If she is in her town house, she could help her maids to air the dresses and furs which are stored in the great chests, and try to remove any stains or fleas.

At about 10 a.m. the household has dinner – the main meal of the day. After dinner, the mistress must see that the servants receive their meal, and then she may go out riding, visit her female friends, or spend some time in the garden. This recreation should be followed by a period spent sewing or spinning with the maidservants of the house.

In the evening, the master of the house returns, and there may be guests for supper. As night falls, the final task of the day is to check that all the doors are locked, all candles have been extinguished, and all the servants have gone to bed.

SOURCE 8 A day in the life of the wife of a small farmer

First set all things in good order within the house, milk the cows, feed the calves, strain the milk, get corn and malt ready for the mill to bake and to brew. You should make butter and cheese and feed the pigs both morning and evening. Keep an eye on how the hens, ducks and geese are laying, and protect their chicks from rats and foxes. If a husband has sheep, his wife may have some of the wool to make clothes, or blankets or coverlets or both.

It is a wife's job to separate the corn from the chaff, and in time of need to help her husband to fill the muck wagon or dung cart, drive the plough, to load hay, corn and such other. Also to go to the market, to sell butter, cheese, milk, eggs, chickens, hens, pigs, geese, and all manner of corn. And also to buy all manner of necessary things belonging to the household, and to give a true account to her husband of what she has received and what she has paid.

4. Look at Sources 9, 10 and 11. Write a description of what you think is or has been happening to the couples in each picture.
5. Imagine you are the author of either Source 7 or Source 8. Write a few more sentences of advice in the same style to help wives know what to do in the situations shown in Sources 9, 10 and 11.

SOURCE 9 From a fifteenth-century manuscript

SOURCE 10 From a fifteenth-century manuscript

SOURCE 11 From a fifteenth-century manuscript

Childbirth

Sources 7 and 8 did not mention children. Yet most women when they got married would have expected to have children. There was no reliable contraception (except to avoid sex altogether), so many women found themselves pregnant, even when they did not want to be.

For both rich and poor having children was a risk. Childbirth was the most common cause of death among women in their teens and twenties. If there were complications in the birth, an operation such as a Caesarian section was very dangerous and would usually result in the death of the mother. There were no painkilling drugs, and it was difficult to stop the bleeding. About one in every five births resulted in the death of the mother.

Claude de France was married when she was fourteen. She had her first child when she was fifteen. In all, she had seven children in nine years.

Seven children was unusual even for a rich woman. However, wealthier women did tend to have more children than peasants. This was because they married younger, had a better diet and did not feed their babies themselves. Instead, they paid women known as 'wet-nurses' to feed their babies for them. They therefore did not have the contraceptive protection that comes from breast-feeding. On average, rich women had four children.

For rich women childbirth was surrounded by ritual and ceremony. Four to six weeks before the baby was born the mother 'took to her chamber'. She would then stay there until forty days after the birth, when she would be taken to church for a special ceremony to clean and purify her. This would be followed by feasting and celebration, after which the woman was able to return to her normal role in the household.

SOURCE 12 A midwife and several ladies help at the birth of a noblewoman's child

Poorer women, such as **Martha**, did not have large numbers of children – two were typical. There are many reasons for this. They married later, often in their late twenties, which cut short the period of childbearing. Martha would have had her children in her early thirties. Peasant women also breast-fed their babies for eighteen months or more, and this, combined with their poor diet, served as a form of contraception, because women are less likely to become pregnant while they are breast-feeding. There were also many miscarriages, still-births and, perhaps, deliberate abortions.

Martha would have been helped in the birth of her children by a midwife, who might have been the wise-woman in her village, or by friends or members of her family. She would have been back at work as soon after the birth as possible.

Motherhood

Looking after children was seen as a woman's job, rather than a man's. How did the responsibilities of childcare affect women's lives?

Once the children of rich families were born, the mother would not take a very active part in looking after them. Wet-nurses would take care of the babies, while servants, teachers and governesses looked after the older children.

Claude might actually have seen very little of her young children. Indeed, the sort of life described in Source 7 might have been very little changed by the arrival of children.

For Martha, on the other hand, childcare would have become part of her everyday life. She would have tried to fit the childcare around her many other tasks (see Source 8 on page 15). One poem from the Middle Ages describes a woman driving the oxen which pulled a plough, while her child lies swaddled (wrapped in tight bands) in the furrows behind her, to prevent it crawling off. However, other members of her family would have been available to help out. Her husband might well have been involved. And just as Martha as a child had been expected to care for a younger sister or brother, so she would have expected her older child to help look after her new baby.

Motherhood could have its frustrations and difficulties. The court records reveal that for some women the pressures of family life were too great.

They show how women sometimes killed themselves, or killed their husbands or children. Margaret Calbot knifed her two-year-old daughter to death, and then threw her four-year-old son on to the fire. A Northamptonshire woman whipped her ten-year-old child to death, and in 1316 Emma le Bere killed her children by cutting their throats with an axe. She then hanged herself.

▲SOURCE 13 An engraving called 'The Bad Upbringing'

▶ SOURCE 14 A medieval picture of a mother calling after a child

Old age and widowhood

Divorce was rare in the Middle Ages. Even if a woman did not like her husband, she had to stay with him. The usual way that marriages ended was with the death of one partner. However, people did not live as long as they do today, and, if they survived childbirth, women tended to live longer than men. So it was not unusual for a woman in her forties to find herself a widow.

If a woman did live longer than her husband, widowhood could bring about an enormous change in her social position. She might have lost the love and security of her marriage, but for the first time she became legally independent. For the first time she could make her own decisions.

Claude de France died at the age of twenty-four after the birth of her seventh child. She never experienced widowhood.

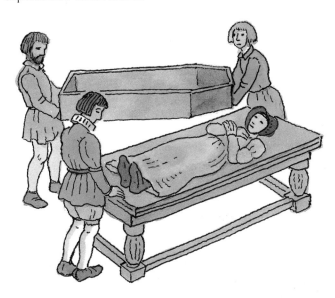

As a widow **Martha** would be allowed to hold land and own property for the first time. She could keep all her husband's land, as long as she was able to perform the labour service due to the lord.

If she had a son a widow might reach an agreement with him to help her. For example, in 1281 Thomas Bird of Romsley took over his mother's cottage. In return he

promised to maintain her 'fully and honourably so long as she shall live'. He agreed to build her a 'competent dwelling . . . thirty feet in length within the walls, and fourteen feet in breadth, with corner posts and three new and competent doors and two windows'. She would have ample food, as well as 'five cart-loads of sea coal' per year.

Martha's widow's rights might have had conditions attached. For example, in some places a widow's rights were only upheld as long as she did not take a new sexual partner. At Enborne, in Berkshire, the manor court declared that if a woman had sex she would lose her property and status as a widow. She could, however, be forgiven if she were prepared to appear before the next meeting of the court, riding backwards on a black ram, with its tail in her hand, saying:

'Here I am,
Riding upon a Black Ram.
Like a whore as I am;
And for my Crincum Crancum,
Have lost my Bincum Bancum;
And for my Tail's game
Am brought to this Worldly Shame.'

There are no records of manors where men were expected to undergo similar ceremonies!

The widows of tradesmen and craftsmen often continued their husband's businesses, sometimes with the help of an assistant. Some became prosperous and successful independent women. Others used their independence to choose a new husband for themselves and remarried.

Activity

Work in pairs.

Imagine you are preparing a family album for either Claude or Martha.

Using drawings and descriptions, make a suitable entry for each stage of their lives: childhood, marriage, childbirth, motherhood, widowhood.

How did the Church treat women?

IN THE Middle Ages the most powerful influence on people's attitudes and behaviour was the Church.

Every village in medieval Britain had a church. The church and its priest were at the centre of village life.

The Church had courts that controlled many aspects of people's lives, such as whom they could marry, whether they could divorce and who should inherit a dead person's property.

The Church was also very rich. It owned a lot of land and villagers paid taxes, or tithes, to the Church.

Regular church services on Sundays and saints' days brought the people of the village together. It was also the Church that taught people how they should behave and what they should think. Ordinary people believed that if they obeyed the priest and lived as the Church said, they might avoid the terrors and tortures awaiting them in hell and get to heaven instead.

The Church was therefore a powerful influence not only on people's behaviour but also on their attitudes and ideas. If we can find out what the Church taught about women, we will be taking steps towards understanding what many people in Britain in the Middle Ages believed about women's role.

At the heart of everything was the Bible's teaching that women should obey their husbands. The Bible says that a woman should not argue with her husband or be proud. The Church taught that men were not only stronger than women, but better at making decisions, and that men had better minds. Read Source 1, for example.

SOURCE 1 Written by Gratian, a Church leader, in 1140

" *The natural order is that women should serve men, for it is just that the lesser serve the greater.*

Woman's authority is nil; let her in all things be subject to the rule of man . . . neither can she teach, nor be a witness [in court], nor sit in judgement. "

Not only should a wife be obedient, but she should also be chaste (not give in to sexual desires or needs). She should certainly be faithful to her husband (not have sex with another man).

This kind of woman – according to the Church – should be praised and admired. Every man should be proud to have such a wife.

The bad woman, on the other hand, was the one who broke these basic rules. She was disobedient and wanted to have control of affairs. According to the Church, if a woman did not obey a man then there was no knowing what might happen. With their great beauty and sexual attraction, disobedient women could tempt men to do

wrong. This kind of woman, said the Church, should be feared and despised.

These two extremes were presented to ordinary people through two stories from the Bible, the stories of Eve (the bad woman) and Mary (the good woman). These stories influenced how people saw women in the Middle Ages.

Activity

As you read the stories and study the pictures of these two women in Sources 2–7, think about the image of the ideal woman that is being presented. For example, which of the following words could you use to describe Eve and which to describe Mary:

- sinful
- pure
- curious
- motherly
- dangerous

- sexual
- content
- ambitious
- greedy
- cautious?

Eve – the first woman

According to the Bible, God created Adam (the first man) and Eve (the first woman) and put them into the Garden of Eden. He gave them only one rule about what to do in the Garden – that they should not eat the fruit of 'the Tree of Knowledge'. Otherwise, He left them to themselves.

In the Garden of Eden everything was perfect. Adam and Eve looked after the plants and animals, but the work was not too hard. Adam and Eve got on well together. They were naked, but they were not embarrassed. Nothing ever went wrong.

Then along came trouble in the form of a snake . . .

Source 2 is a ninth-century painting of the story. It is a bit like a cartoon strip.

---

1. Match the descriptions below to the parts of the story shown in Source 2.
   Descriptions
   God creates Adam and Eve
   God tells them not to eat from the Tree of Knowledge
   Eve is tempted by the snake to eat the fruit
   Eve persuades Adam to eat the fruit, too
   When God finds out, Adam blames Eve
   God expels them from the Garden
   Eve's punishment is the pain of bearing children
   Adam's punishment is to have to work hard
2. How have Adam and Eve changed as a result of eating the apple?

SOURCE 3 From a sermon by Geoffrey of Vendôme, a Norman bishop, in 1095

Do you not know that you are Eve, too? You are the door the Devil uses to get in. You have agreed to eat from the forbidden tree. You were the first to reject the rules of God.

SOURCE 4 Written by Gratian in 1140

Adam was tempted by Eve, not she by him. It is right that he whom woman led into wrongdoing should have her under his direction, so that he may not fail a second time through female weakness.

Other Church writers took an even sterner and more vicious line. St John Chrysostom said 'Among all savage beasts, none is found as harmful as woman.' Others compared women with foul substances, as you can see in Source 5.

SOURCE 5 Written by Odo of Cluny in the tenth century

Physical beauty is only skin deep. If men could see beneath the skin, the sight of women would make them nauseous. We are loath to touch spittle or dung even with our finger tips; how can we desire to embrace a sack of dung?

As soon as they disobeyed God, Adam and Eve became embarrassed about being naked and covered their bodies with leaves. According to the Bible, it was only then, when they had already sinned, that Adam and Eve had sex. The clear message was that sex is also dangerous and sinful.

The Church presented Eve in this story as the disobedient woman who created all these problems and ruined everything for the whole human race.

Men and women – according to the Church – lost their perfect life because of a woman's weakness.

As well as throwing them out of the Garden, the Bible says that God punished Adam and Eve in other ways. He announced His curse: men would have to work hard to grow enough food to stay alive, and women would suffer pain in childbirth.

All this misery was supposed to have come from the failings of the first woman. If Eve was responsible for this great mistake, said the Church, men must beware of women. You can see the views of Church leaders in Sources 3–5.

1. What do Sources 1–5 suggest about the way the medieval Church viewed
a) women?
b) sex?

Mary – the mother of Jesus

If Eve was at one extreme, Mary was at the other. As the mother of Jesus she helped solve the problems caused by Eve.

According to the Bible, Mary was an ordinary young woman, yet God decided that she should become the mother of Jesus, who would be saviour of the world. Source 6 is from the Bible. It describes the moment when an angel came to Mary and gave her the news.

> **SOURCE 6** From the Bible: Luke, chapter 1
>
> " *The angel said: 'Don't be afraid, Mary; God has chosen you. You will become pregnant and give birth to a son and you will name him Jesus. The Lord God will make him a king; his kingdom will never end.'*
>
> *Mary said to the angel, 'I am a virgin. How can this be?'*
>
> *The angel answered, 'The Holy Spirit will come on you and God's power will rest on you.'*
>
> *'I am the Lord's servant,' said Mary.* "

For the people of the Middle Ages, Mary had all the qualities of the ideal woman. Source 7 shows Mary as the perfect mother, with a strong bond with her child and her husband. Source 6 shows her as a pure virgin who is unspoiled by sex, and an obedient servant, ready to do what God wanted – the opposite of the self-willed Eve.

Mary was presented as the opposite of Eve in every way:

■ Eve disobeyed God; Mary obeyed God.

■ Eve had sexual desires; Mary was a virgin.

■ Eve brought suffering into the world; Mary brought hope.

For the people of the Middle Ages these images were intense and powerful. Through them the Church made sure that ordinary women were in no doubt about what was expected of them: to avoid the weaknesses of Eve and to copy the virtues of Mary – obedience, virginity and care of the family. Look back at Source 4 on page 13. Mary is shown as Claude's teacher and companion.

The Church was very successful in its presentation of Mary. Ordinary people took to the idea very eagerly. During the Middle Ages Mary was raised to a status almost as great as that of Jesus himself. Local churches adopted Mary as their saint; even today you can still find many churches dedicated to her. Thousands of pictures were painted of her. People prayed to her, and every church in the country would have a chapel or altar with a statue of Mary overlooking the congregation and giving them her blessing.

Hundreds of thousands of people made pilgrimages to places associated with Mary.

SOURCE 7 The Holy Family – a painting from the Middle Ages

SOURCE 8 A painting of Mary and the baby Jesus in a church

What role could women have in the Church?

The Church was dominated by men. The Pope, the bishops and all the priests were men. The rules were made by men. Nearly all the religious books were written by men.

Yet religion was as important to many women as it was to men. Men expected women to be content with trying to be more like Mary and less like Eve. But some women wanted to play a more active part in the Church. How could they have a role? They were not allowed to become priests because women were seen as the weaker sex, who had to be controlled by men. If they were going to serve the Church they had to find other ways of doing it.

Some wealthy women became **benefactors**. During their lives, or in their wills, they gave money to the Church to pay for priests or church buildings. Another possibility for women in the Middle Ages was to become a nun.

Nuns

Nuns cut themselves off from contact with the world and gave their lives to God.

Nuns lived together in a nunnery, a convent or a priory. There were about eighty nunneries in medieval Britain. The nuns prayed, looked after the poor and grew food in the fields and gardens attached to the nunnery.

Women became nuns for different reasons. For example:
■ Some wanted to avoid marriage and childbirth. One nun, Christina, who became head of the nunnery at Markyate, became a nun to escape having to marry the man her parents had chosen.
■ Some women were put into a nunnery by parents who were unable to find husbands for them.

Activity

In the Middle Ages one of the most popular ways of teaching religious ideas was the 'mystery play'. In the mystery plays actors would act out stories from the Bible. They would travel from village to village, performing these plays from the back of a wagon. Your teacher can give you an information sheet about mystery plays with examples of the dramas they performed.

The first story in the series would usually be about the creation of the world and Adam and Eve. The last story might be about Mary and the birth of Jesus.

Work in two groups. One group should prepare a two-minute mystery play to begin the series. In your play, make it clear what your audience should think of Eve. The other group should prepare a mystery play to end the series. In your play, make it clear what your audience should think of Mary.

HOW DID THE CHURCH TREAT WOMEN?

■ Some women became nuns because they wanted to give their lives to God.

Some nunneries were very small, with just three or four nuns living together. Others were quite large. There were nunneries that were poor and where the nuns lived quite hard lives. Others were wealthy and the nuns lived comfortably.

Most nuns came from well-off families. Even in a wealthy nunnery, if you were poor and had no income of your own life would be very hard. Very few poor women became nuns.

Nuns had to be able to read in order to use their Bibles and prayer books. For this reason, nuns were usually better educated than other women – indeed, being in a nunnery was one of the few ways that a woman could receive an education in the Middle Ages. Wealthy families sometimes sent their young children to live and be educated in a monastery.

Some nuns became quite powerful. Isabella of Lancaster was the niece of King Edward I. She was educated in a nunnery, then became a nun herself and eventually ran her own nunnery. She travelled widely and used her influence with the king and her own family to improve the nunnery.

Nunneries fitted in very well with what male Church leaders thought women should be doing. They didn't mind nuns learning to read, because they were using that skill to worship God. Nuns also lived a chaste and pure life, just like Mary. Unlike Mary, they did not have a husband or children to look after, but they were expected instead to be 'married to God' and to treat him as their family.

SOURCE 10 Nuns singing in choir

SOURCE 9 written by a French cardinal, who visited many convents

“ I saw banded together, many holy virgins who despised the attractions of the flesh and the riches of the world for the sake of the kingdom of heaven. Clinging in poverty and humility to their heavenly Husband [God], they earned a meagre living with the labour of their hands, yet they came from very rich families. ”

SOURCE 11 A thirteenth-century poem which was very popular in convents around Europe. The poem is about the life of Mary. In this extract Mary is expressing what many nuns felt about God

“ You are my father, you are my brother.
You are my sister, you are my mother.
You are my husband, you are my lord.
You are my keeper and my comforter.
You are my bridegroom, to you I give my virginity.
You are my handsome husband; I long to be with you always.
You are my lover and my friend: I'm set on fire by your love. ”

▲ **SOURCE 12** Nuns nursing sick people

◀ **SOURCE 13**
The nuns' daily
routine

▲**SOURCE 15** Nuns in the
refectory

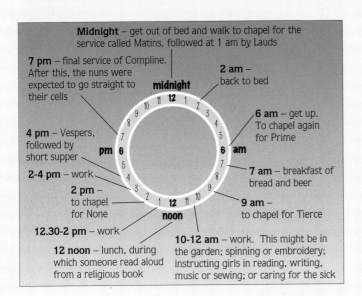

Midnight – get out of bed and walk to chapel for the
service called Matins, followed at 1 am by Lauds

7 pm – final service of Compline.
After this, the nuns were
expected to go straight to
their cells

2 am –
back to bed

6 am – get up.
To chapel again
for Prime

4 pm – Vespers,
followed by
short supper

7 am – breakfast of
bread and beer

2-4 pm – work

2 pm –
to chapel
for None

9 am –
to chapel for Tierce

12.30-2 pm – work

10-12 am – work. This might be in
the garden; spinning or embroidery;
instructing girls in reading, writing,
music or sewing; or caring for the sick

12 noon – lunch, during
which someone read aloud
from a religious book

▶ **SOURCE 16**
A nun in her
private room.
These were
called cells

SOURCE 14 Written by modern historian Eileen
Power in *Medieval Women*

❝*It is impossible to deny that nunneries were a help
for women in the Middle Ages.*

*To unmarried gentlewomen they gave scope to
abilities which might otherwise have run to waste,
giving them self-respect and the respect of society.*

*They made use of women's powers of organisation
in running communities and managing households
and estates.*

*They gave nuns the chance of a good education
and spiritual experience.*

*The nunneries represented an honourable
profession and fulfilled a useful function, for
gentlewomen of the Middle Ages.*❞

1. The life of a medieval nun was very different from
   the life of a medieval gentlewoman and that of
   the wife of a small farmer (Sources 7 and 8 on
   page 15). Which of the three lives would you
   prefer? Make a list of your reasons.
2. Read Source 14. Do you agree with Eileen
   Power? Support your answer with evidence from
   pages 23–25 of this book.

How do we find out about sixteenth- and seventeenth-century women?

YOU are now going to move on in your study of the changing role of women to look at the sixteenth and seventeenth centuries.

In many ways, in the sixteenth and seventeenth centuries women's lives remained much the same as they had been in the Middle Ages:

■ Their lives were still governed by the same cycle of marriage, childbirth and childcare.

■ Their work remained much the same. It was still based in the home. Women combined childcare and housework with work in the family's fields, in the family business or with extra paid work of their own.

In the seventeenth century the majority of women still lived in the country, in their parents' or husband's cottage. They still did a variety of different sorts of work. They brewed beer at home. They spun and weaved at home – in fact, many more women did this now, as the wool industry was growing very quickly. Some women did other jobs at home, such as making hats, sewing gloves or making lace. The number of middle-class families was growing, but even in these richer families women's lives were still dominated by having and rearing children and by household duties.

However, there is one thing that is really different about the sixteenth and seventeenth centuries: the increased amount of evidence that has survived and is available to us.

Whereas the problem facing the historian of the Middle Ages was how to find any evidence at all about women's lives, the problem facing historians of the sixteenth and seventeenth centuries is how to interpret all the different evidence that is available.

Remember, however, that it is still the rich, educated, wealthy and powerful women that we know most about. Peasant women could not read or write, so they did not write letters or keep diaries. They could not afford to have an artist paint their portrait. They had fewer possessions and those they had did not usually survive.

---

1. Look at Source 1. What aspects of women's lives do you think this extra evidence might help us to find out more about? As a class, list as many things it will help with as possible.
2. Are there things it might not help with?
3. Having a lot of evidence about a period can sometimes be as big a problem for a historian as having little evidence. Make a list of problems caused by having lots of evidence about a period.

Private life

One area where the extra evidence is most helpful is for finding out about women's private lives or their family lives. Letters, journals, diaries, paintings and objects give us information about women's lives, including about their feelings and reactions, that we could not get from official sources such as court records or tax returns.

For example, Sources 2–16 give us details about a range of things, such as:

■ women's household duties
■ their relationships with men
■ their attitude to God
■ their possessions
■ the dangers of travel in this period.

SOURCE 1 Sixteenth- and seventeenth-century evidence about the lives of women

SOURCE 2 The Saltonstall family, painted in about 1641

SOURCE 4 The title page of Richard Brathwait's book *The English Gentleman and English Gentlewoman*, published in 1631

Activity

Your task is to prepare a class display which presents a picture of women's lives in this period. You will be using Sources 2–16. This is a suggested way of working.

1. Work in groups. Each group works on different headings from the list at the end of page 26.
2. In the centre of a large sheet of paper or card put the heading, one heading per sheet.
3. Decide which of Sources 2–16 help you find out about that aspect of women's lives.
4. Summarise what you have found out from each source around the large sheet.
5. Do the same for any other aspects you are looking at.
6. Put the finished sheets together as a class display.

SOURCE 3 The will of Martha Barton, a widow, who lived in Combs in Suffolk, 7 May 1630. The range of possessions shows that she was not poor

❝ *I give to my daughters Margaret and Martha my chest of linen to be equally divided between them.*

I give to Margaret the bedstead in the chamber next to the hall. Also to her the lesser of my two brass pots and two brass candlesticks.

I give to Martha Fellgate [grandchild] the bed in the parlour with bedding.

I give to my daughter Margaret six pieces of my best pewter . . . the biggest brass kettle but one and the chest in the parlour.

I give to my daughter Martha the cupboard and table in the parlour.

I give to the poor of Combs forty shillings. ❞

SOURCE 5 Written by a male Dutch visitor to England in 1575

❝ *Wives in England are entirely in the power of their husbands, yet they are not kept so strictly as in Spain. Nor are they shut up.*

They go to market. They are well dressed, fond of taking it easy and leave the care of the household to their servants.

They spend time walking and riding, playing cards and visiting friends, talking to neighbours and making merry with them, and in childbirths and christenings. All this with the permission of their husbands. This is why England is called the paradise of married women. ❞

Activity

In the original of Source 4 each of the pictures had a caption summarising the ideal qualities of a gentleman or gentlewoman. We have blanked them out. Work with a partner to decide what quality each one shows. On your own copy of Source 4, which you can get from your teacher, add the captions. Your teacher will tell you if you are right.

Are the qualities of the ideal woman similar to those of women:
a) in the Middle Ages?
b) today?

SOURCE 6 From the diary of Elizabeth Mordaunt in 1657. She had just discovered that she was pregnant

O Lord, do thou assist me in the condition I am now in. Preserve the child within me, the time it has to stay, from every ill accident, and when my hour of labour comes, let thy holy angels be assisting. Grant me a safe delivery; support me in my greatest extremity; and bless my child with perfect shape; make it beautiful in body and mind; and receive both that and me, and all mine, into thy Almighty protection, now and for ever more.

SOURCE 7 Extracts from Lady Margaret Hoby's diary, giving details of her activities for the week from 4 to 11 April 1601. She lived in Yorkshire. Her marriage to Thomas Hoby was her third marriage

April 4 I was almost all afternoon in the garden sowing seed, where Mr Bushill [a neighbour] came to see us. After, I returned in to my Chamber, and there read and prayed till I went to supper.

April 5 – Sunday Having prayed I broke my fast and then went to church, where, having heard the sermon . . . I returned home, and privately gave thanks to God.

After the afternoon sermon [at church], I spent the rest of the day reading, singing, praying.

April 6 Having prayed as usual, I sewed in the house with my maids all the afternoon, till I went to private meditation and prayer.

April 7 After praying and reading I kept Mr Gatt [her cousin] company.

After dinner I sewed and heard Mr Rhodes read. I sent away [dismissed] Besse Stafford [probably a servant]. After, I walked with my husband, and then returned to private prayer.

April 8 Mr Hoby was gone to York. I read and sewed a while before dinner. After, I went with my maids into the garden.

April 9 This day I continued to praise God, without sickness or trouble: and so, like wise, the 10 and 11 day.

April 11 After private prayers I was busy in the kitchen and garden until Mr Hoby came home. After I had walked a little, I went to private prayers.

SOURCE 8 A letter written by Brilliana Lady Harley in 1642. During the Civil War, her husband and her son Ned were in London, leaving her to defend the family home in Herefordshire against Royalist soldiers, who were besieging it

My deare Ned, I should have been very glad to have received a letter from you, that I might know how it is with your father and yourself, for it is a death to be amongst my enemies and not heare from those I love so dearly.

They say that if I do not give them my house and the things they want that I will be proceeded against as a traitor. I believe everyone will be as unwilling to part with their house as I am. I desire that your father would seriously think what I had best do.

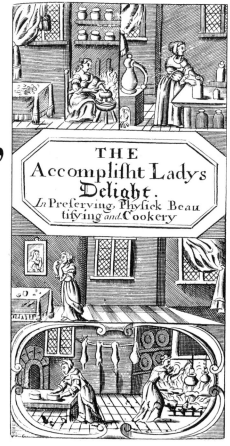

▲**SOURCE 9** A seventeenth-century pamphlet, *The Accomplished Lady's Delight*

SOURCE 10 From a census of the poor in Norwich

Ann Buckle, 46 year old. Widow. Two children one nine years old, the other five years old, that work lace. Have always lived here. Very poor.

1. Study Source 10. Look for the following information and compare it with the life of Martha in the Middle Ages (pages 13–14 and 17–19):
   a) Ann Buckle's age when she had her children
   b) how many children she had
   c) how widowhood affected her.

SOURCE 12 Extracts from the diary of Mary Rich, Countess of Warwick

30 January 1667 My husband fell into a mood and provoked me to a dispute. I was kept from saying anything unfit, but was troubled by his unkindness and wept much, though I did not come to any quarrel with him. I determined not to argue and to bear all his passionate, provoking expressions.

15 March 1667 My brother Hatton Rich dined with us. He did dreadfully swear and talked so ill I thought nothing out of hell could have done. I did all I could to keep him from it, did show my dislike at it . . .

My husband was exceedingly angry with Daniel Shirley [a servant]. I strove to take him off from it, but he fell violently angry against me, which made me, wicked wretch that I was, speak angry words softly to myself unadvisedly with my lips; and, O Lord, though no man heard them, Thou didst, therefore pardon Thy unworthy servant.

I fell into a foolish dispute with my husband in which I was too earnest and too passionate, and continued to be so a good while, but afterwards, before I went to bed, I was much troubled at it, and did beg God's pardon for my wickedness.

SOURCE 13 From Celia Fiennes' account of her travels around Britain, written in the 1680s. She travelled on horseback with two servants and a greyhound to every county in England and to the borders of Scotland and Wales. This incident took place in Shropshire

As we rode through a wood two men all of a sudden joined us from the wood. They looked loaded up . . . with pistols. They dogged me, one in front, the other behind, and jostled my horse to get between my servant's horse and mine. But the Goodness of God so arranged it that it being market day at Whitchurch I was continually meeting market people so the men called each other off and left us.

◄ **SOURCE 14** A wedding feast in Bermondsey in the 1600s

Activity

Your teacher will give you a set of books about the sixteenth and seventeenth centuries.

Repeat the exercise that you did for the Middle Ages (see page 11).

Compare your findings about this period with your findings about the Middle Ages. Is there more information about women's lives in books on this period or less?

How do you explain your findings?

◄ **SOURCE 15** A woman serving in a London coffee shop in the seventeenth century

Mary and Elizabeth

In THE 1560s both England and Scotland were ruled by women, even though at this time women were excluded from almost all political life.

Over the next four pages you are going to investigate how people at the time reacted to these two women, and how people since then have interpreted their lives. Were Mary and Elizabeth judged in the same way that a king would have been judged? Do the changing interpretations of Mary and Elizabeth's lives tell us anything about the changing role of women?

What happened?

Elizabeth I was Queen of England from 1558 to 1603, while her cousin Mary Stuart was Queen of Scotland from 1561 to 1567. It was a time of great tension and rivalry between England and Scotland and the two queens, although they were cousins, became bitter rivals.

Elizabeth was a Protestant, but Mary was a Catholic. Mary's Catholic supporters plotted to get rid of Elizabeth. They wanted to make Mary Queen of England as well as Scotland and to make England a Catholic country.

Mary became Elizabeth's prisoner and eventually – under pressure from her closest advisers – Elizabeth had Mary executed. Your teacher can give you a sheet telling the story if you want to know more.

How were they seen in the sixteenth century?

In the sixteenth century women were expected to obey men, not to rule them.

What did people at the time make of these two powerful women?

There is plenty of evidence for us to look at. There are thousands of letters, paintings and memoirs, including Sources 1–8.

---

1. Which of Sources 1–9:
   a) praise Mary
   b) praise Elizabeth
   c) criticise Mary
   d) criticise Elizabeth?
2. What are the two women praised for?
3. What are they criticised for?

SOURCE 2 A paraphrase of a French poem written by one of Mary's friends in the 1550s

Her form and her face outshine even her intellect.

In her, such grace combines with such majesty that you'd think her body was that of a god.

Nor does she lack the high gifts of wisdom. Her powers of judgement are greater than you would expect of someone of her sex and her age.

SOURCE 1 Roger Ascham was Elizabeth's private teacher. He wrote this about the young Elizabeth

Her mind has no womanly weakness, her perseverance is equal to that of a man, and her memory long keeps what it quickly picks up. I am inventing nothing . . . there is no need.

When we look at sources like these it is essential to remember their background. The rivalry between Scotland and England, and between the Catholics and the Protestants, affected the way both monarchs were represented.

Elizabeth's friends and advisers praised Elizabeth. Mary's friends and advisers, naturally, praised Mary. Even portraits of the two women were designed to show them in the best possible way.

SOURCE 3 The execution of Mary Queen of Scots, painted by an unknown artist

---

4. Look at Sources 4 and 7. It was the job of a portrait painter to make a monarch look impressive. How did the painter try to make Elizabeth look impressive? What qualities did the artist emphasise in his portrait of Mary?

▲SOURCE 4 A portrait of Mary Queen of Scots painted for her friend and servant Elizabeth Curle

▲SOURCE 7 A portrait of Queen Elizabeth painted in 1588 to commemorate the British defeat of the Spanish Armada

SOURCE 5 The English Parliament's judgement on Mary when it was demanding that she be executed

The Queen of Scots is hardened in malice and bent upon destruction of Her Majesty [Elizabeth]. She is a fierce, hard and desperate woman. As long as she lives Her Majesty will never be safe. She is poisoned with Popery [Catholicism] and is burning to destroy [Protestantism] in England and everywhere.

SOURCE 6 Written by John Knox, a Scottish Protestant and a strong opponent of the Catholic Mary

written when Mary was made queen

To promote a woman to bear rule is unnatural, against God's will and subverts good order and justice . . . All men lamented that the country was left without a man to become king.

written after his first meeting with Mary

If there is not a proud mind, a crafty wit, and a hard heart against God and his truth, my judgement fails me.

SOURCE 8 Written by Molino, an Italian visitor to England, in 1607, shortly after Elizabeth's death

Elizabeth was the most remarkable princess that has appeared in the world for these many centuries. In all her actions she displayed the greatest carefulness, which is evident from the fact that she reigned forty-two years and kept her kingdom in peace, though at the start it was full of bad feeling. But she knew how to adapt to circumstances so well that she overcame every difficulty. With her firmness she not only withstood her enemies but overpowered them.

She was beloved by her subjects, who still miss her; she was dreaded by her enemies; and in a word possessed, in the highest degree, all the qualities which are required in a great prince.

Judgements on their reigns

When Mary was executed on Elizabeth's orders in 1588, her short reign had reached its disastrous end.

Elizabeth, on the other hand, had a long reign. While she was queen, England became a richer and more stable country, won important battles with other countries and began to develop an overseas empire.

As a political leader, Mary was seen at the time as a failure, whereas Elizabeth was seen as a successful and skilful politician.

We are now going to investigate whether these interpretations changed in later centuries.

MARY AND ELIZABETH

The nineteenth-century view

In the nineteenth century there was a new interest in Elizabeth and Mary, and people began to have different views to those of earlier writers.

One historian, James Froude, wrote a bestselling history of Britain. He was in no doubt that under Queen Elizabeth England became a great nation, but he seemed doubtful whether Elizabeth herself was responsible for this success.

He concluded that all the successes of Elizabeth's reign were, in fact, the work of Lord Burghley, one of her advisers.

> **SOURCE 9** Written by James Froude in 1870
>
> "It is more and more clear to me that Burghley was the author of Elizabeth and England's greatness.
> She never chose an opposite course without plunging into embarrassment from which his skill was barely able to extricate her."

Froude also had new opinions on Mary. Source 10 is another extract from his book.

> **SOURCE 10**
>
> "Never did human creature meet death more bravely . . .
> In form and grace Mary Stuart had the advantage of her rival everywhere. Elizabeth could stoop to mean manoeuvres. Mary Stuart carried herself with a majesty which would have become the noblest of sovereigns."

Other nineteenth-century writers and artists looked at the two queens in a similar way. The conflict between Elizabeth and Mary began to be written about not as a political or religious conflict, but as a personal clash between different 'types' of woman.

Elizabeth was seen as a hard-hearted woman, with characteristics that were thought to be 'masculine'. Mary, on the other hand, had the qualities every nineteenth-century woman was supposed to have, as Source 11 shows.

The story of Mary appealed to Victorian readers. Books about her became immensely popular, and she was seen as a tragic and romantic heroine.

Engravings such as Source 12 were published regularly throughout the century. In writing and pictures Mary was celebrated for her beauty, her weakness in love, and her pious and brave death.

> 1. Compare Source 12 with Source 3 on page 30. They cannot both be right. How do you explain the differences between the pictures?

> **SOURCE 11** From the introduction by Mrs P. Stewart-Mackenzie Arbuthnot to *Queen Mary's Book*, 1907
>
> "In the game of worldly prosperity, Elizabeth won and Mary lost; but when we look at the matter closely, and consider which of the two women was richer in the qualities that bring true happiness, does Mary need our pity after all?
> We find she had friends who were capable of dying cheerfully in her cause, or suffering for nineteen years in captivity for her sake. We find she was worshipped by children and loved by animals. We find she was able to forgive not only her enemies, but her friends.
> Christianity has no more crucial test than this. And we find that she died with a calm heroism rarely, if ever, equalled in the history of her sex."

SOURCE 12 The execution of Mary, Queen of Scots, by Robert Herdman (1867). The light on Mary's head gives her a saintly quality that reinforces the idea of her as a brave martyr

> ### Activity
>
> You have been asked by a nineteenth-century magazine to write an article about Mary, Queen of Scots. Source 12 will be used to illustrate it.
>
> Write a short article, comparing her with Elizabeth, then write a caption for the illustration.

The twentieth-century view

In the twentieth century there have been more changes in the interpretation of Mary and Elizabeth's lives.

With the increasing involvement of women in politics, the two queens were judged more on their performance as politicians than on their personalities.

While Mary had been the more popular figure in the nineteenth century, in the twentieth century there was once again much more attention focused on Elizabeth. Since the rise of feminism and Margaret Thatcher's long term of office as Prime Minister (1979–1990), there has been increasing interest in how Elizabeth used power, and what having power did to her.

> **SOURCE 13** Written by Susan Bassnett in *Elizabeth I: A Feminist Perspective* in 1988
>
> " *Far from being an inadequate woman or [almost] a man, Elizabeth should be seen as a woman who struggled against anti-feminist prejudice and who has remained a symbol of female assertiveness for future generations.* "

◀ **SOURCE 14** From the BBC television series *Elizabeth R*. The actress Glenda Jackson, who is now an MP, portrayed Elizabeth as a strong woman, but one who was eventually isolated by her position, which cut her off from other people

▶ **SOURCE 15** A still from the BBC television comedy series *Blackadder*. Miranda Richardson presents Elizabeth as a rather silly young woman, who liked practical jokes and who had people's heads chopped off at a whim

> **SOURCE 16** Written by Jenny Wormald in 1988 in *Mary Queen of Scots: A Study in Failure*
>
> " *Mary was a tragic figure not because she was young and female . . . She was tragic because she was one of the rare cases of someone born to supreme power who was wholly unable to cope with its responsibilities. Mary ended her life a complete failure.* "

> **SOURCE 17** Written by Paul Johnson in 1974 in *Elizabeth I: A Study in Power and Intellect*
>
> " *Mary was unable to play the role of a responsible sovereign. It was the main charge Elizabeth held against her . . . Monarchy involved duties, as well as rights; this was something Mary could never understand. Elizabeth was a professional, Mary a self-willed amateur.* "

1. Sources 13–15 are recent representations of Elizabeth. Do you think this kind of representation affects the way people today see Elizabeth? Explain your answer.

   Here are summaries of four different opinions of Mary or Elizabeth. Choose one of Sources 1–17 to support each viewpoint.

   > Elizabeth was a ruthless and calculating ruler.

   > Mary was a romantic heroine, loved by those who knew her, but brought down by Elizabeth's schemes.

   > Elizabeth was a wise queen, who always bore in mind the needs of the state and her responsibilities as ruler.

   > Mary was a foolish woman, unable to handle her responsibilities.

2. Choose one assessment of Mary and Elizabeth that you agree with from Sources 1–17.

Why were women accused of being witches?

BETWEEN 1550 and 1650 thousands of people in Britain, mostly women, were accused of being witches.

In the Middle Ages people had thought a lot about heaven and hell, but they had not been particularly worried about witches. Now, all of a sudden, people started spotting witches everywhere.

There was such concern about this that witchcraft was made a criminal offence. This meant that rather than being dealt with by the Church, witches were tried in ordinary courts. It also meant that witches could be hanged if they were found guilty.

Sometimes, so many people were accused that the courts could not cope and special courts had to be set up. In some places a 'witch-hunter' was appointed to find witches and prove they were guilty.

Hundreds of those accused were sentenced to death in trials all over England and Scotland.

Sources 1–5 are descriptions of various witch-trials in the sixteenth and seventeenth centuries.

SOURCE 1 The case of Margaret Harkett

Margaret Harkett was a sixty-year-old widow from Stanmore in Middlesex. She was caught picking peas in a neighbour's field without permission. When the neighbour asked her to give back the peas, she became angry and threw them down on the ground. From that time, no peas would grow in the field. A bailiff found her taking wood from his master's land. He hit her, and later he went mad. A neighbour bought a pair of shoes from Margaret, but he did not give her enough money. He later died.

In 1585 Margaret Harkett was executed in London as a witch.

Activity

Work in groups. Read Sources 1–5, taking one case each.

For your case try to work out:
■ Who is accused? Draw up a profile, including details such as their name, how old they are, their sex, their family situation and their social background.
■ Who is accusing them?
■ What are they accused of doing?
■ Did they confess to being a witch?
■ How were they punished?

You will not be able to find all this information for every case, but work out as much as you can.

SOURCE 2 The case of Margaret Flower

In 1612 Francis Manners, Earl of Rutland, lived in Belvoir Castle near Stamford. Among his servants were Joan Flower and her two daughters, Margaret and Philippa. It was rumoured that Joan was a witch – she looked like a witch, and it was claimed that she was a 'malicious atheist' – [that is, that she did not believe in God]. Margaret Flower lived in the castle, where she did the washing and looked after the poultry. She used to steal bits and pieces from her employers, and as a result was eventually dismissed.

Shortly afterwards, the Earl and his wife became ill. Their eldest son, Henry, died, and the younger son, Francis, and his sister, Katherine, also fell ill. The three Flower women were arrested on suspicion of having used witchcraft to punish the Manners family for the dismissal of Margaret. Joan Flower denied all the charges, saying that she hoped that the bread and butter she had just eaten would choke her if she were guilty. At that, she dropped down dead.

Her body was 'carryed to Lincolne Gaole, with a horrible excruciation of soule and body, and was buried at Ancaster'. Her two daughters were tried for witchcraft and hanged.

SOURCE 3 The case of Elizabeth Francis

In 1565 Elizabeth Francis, of Hatfield Peverell in Essex, confessed to Dr Cole and Master Foscus that she had learned the art of witchcraft from her grandmother, who had given her a white spotted cat called Satan. She kept the cat in a basket and fed it on bread and milk.

Elizabeth wanted a flock of sheep, and the cat 'in a strange hollow voice' promised she should have them. It brought her eighteen sheep, but they later disappeared.

Elizabeth was anxious to be married to Andrew Byles, who had previously 'abused' her. He refused to marry her and so she ordered the cat to bewitch him and he died.

When she found she was pregnant, the cat gave her a herb to eat, which destroyed the child. She then married Mr Francis, and when their baby was six months old, Elizabeth ordered the cat to murder it.

Each time the cat did something for her, Elizabeth gave it a drop of her blood. She kept the cat for fifteen or sixteen years, and then gave it to a poor woman in the neighbourhood.

▲SOURCE 7 A witch creating a storm at sea. Stories of witchcraft trials were very popular. The new printing presses made money out of selling pamphlets like this telling the latest sensational witchcraft stories. Sources 6–8 all come from such pamphlets

SOURCE 4   The case of Margery Stanton

Margery Stanton was a poor woman living in Wimbish in Essex who was tried for witchcraft in 1579. She had been to ask Richard Saunders' wife if she could borrow some yeast. The woman refused, and some time later Richard Saunders' child 'was taken vehemently sick, in a marvellous strange manner'. When Robert Cornell's wife turned down Margery's request for milk, she became ill with a great swelling.

SOURCE 5   The case of Margaret Barclay

A Scottish woman, Margaret Barclay, quarrelled with her sister-in-law. In the heat of the moment she uttered various threats. When her brother-in-law was later drowned in a shipwreck, Margaret was accused of witchcraft and tortured. She eventually confessed, but declared as she was taken to be executed that the confession had been forced out of her by torture. She died proclaiming her innocence.

▼SOURCE 6 A seventeenth-century woodcut of a witch. She is standing by a magic circle, making a spell to summon the devil

▲SOURCE 8 Matthew Hopkins, Witchfinder General. He has accused the two women of being witches. The Devil was supposed to come to them in the disguise of these animals with strange names.

Activity

Write a short definition for a sixteenth-century dictionary explaining what the word 'witch' means. Use Sources 1–8 to compile your definition.

Historians have suggested two factors which may explain the increase in accusations of witchcraft during this period.

Factor 1:
Changes in religious beliefs

The sixteenth century was a time of great religious conflict and change. These changes had their effect on ordinary people in England.

Imagine that you are living in a village in the Middle Ages and something terrible happens to you: for example, your only son dies, or your crops fail and you have no food. In the Middle Ages, you would assume that this had happened because *you* were sinful and God was punishing you. You would go to the priest and ask him to forgive you.

When faced by a major disaster, such as the Black Death, whole villages and towns got together and prayed or went on processions to ask for forgiveness. Some people even punished themselves with whips to show God how sorry they were.

Now imagine that you are living in a village in the 1580s. The Catholic Church has been banned because England is now a Protestant country. Catholic beliefs are also banned.

The new Protestant religion tells you that when something goes wrong it is not because **you** have sinned but because the **Devil** is making things go wrong for you. The Devil has followers called witches. He uses them to bring all sorts of trouble to good Christians. They can make people fall ill or die, or can ruin their crops or harm their animals.

Historians believe that people in the sixteenth century were much more aware of witchcraft, therefore. They were on the look-out for witches.

So if something happens to you now, what do you do? You think of someone in your village who might be 'bewitching' you. It might be someone in the village who is odd or ugly, or even someone whom nowadays we would describe as mentally ill. Or you might suspect that someone you have wronged has a grudge against you and is bewitching you or trying to harm you.

Factor 2:
Changes in village life

The second part of the historians' argument is that at the same time as these religious changes were taking place, there were also changes taking place in village life.

The medieval system where everyone worked for the lord and farmed some of his land in return had long since gone. Now nearly everyone worked for wages. It was a case of every family for itself. A much more selfish society was the result. The landowner gave jobs to as many workers as he wanted; the rest had to find work elsewhere or beg. In the fifteenth and sixteenth centuries many landowners evicted poor families from their land because they wanted to use it to graze sheep to supply wool for the growing wool industry.

As a result of these changes, some people in the villages became richer, but the number of poor people increased enormously. Now that there were so many poor people they were seen as a threat, while poor people in turn became angry with those who were better off. Villages were less united and people trusted one another less.

Historians argue that if a poor woman had asked a neighbour for help in the Middle Ages she would have been given it. In the same way, if a dispute between neighbours had arisen in the Middle Ages the manorial court would have dealt with the problem very straightforwardly. In the sixteenth century, however, the poor person would have been turned away, and disputes between neighbours ended up in witch trials.

There are therefore two factors: people looking for witches to blame for their problems, and a breakdown of relationships in the village. If you combine these together you have a possible explanation for the increase in accusations of witchcraft.

1. Look again at the cases in Sources 1–5. Do they provide any evidence to support these viewpoints?
2. From your knowledge of the period, can you think of other factors which might have made people more interested in witchcraft? Look for example at Source 7 on the previous page.

Why were most accusations made against women?

The accusations in Sources 1–5 are typical of the many witchcraft trials held during the sixteenth and seventeenth centuries. The overwhelming majority of those accused were women. Most commonly the accused women were also old and living alone. Why was this?

Male writers from the time thought hard about why more women were accused than men. Sources 9–11 are some of their conclusions.

SOURCE 9 From a late fifteenth-century account of witchcraft

As for the question, why a greater number of witches is found in the fragile female sex than among men . . . we may add that since they are feebler both in mind and body than men, it is not surprising that they should come more under the spell of witchcraft . . .

SOURCE 10 From a sixteenth-century French work by Jean Bodin

" *It is clear from the books of everyone who has written about witches, that for every male witch there are fifty female witches . . . In my opinion this is not because of the weakness of women – for most of them are extremely obstinate – it is more likely to be because of their great lust.* "

SOURCE 11 From an English book on witchcraft written in 1584 by Reginald Scot, a witch-hunter

" *The reason why women are oftener found to be witches than men:*

Women have a terrible temper so that it is not possible for them to control themselves. Like brute beasts they fix their furious eyes upon the person who they believe has done them wrong and they bewitch them. And of all other women, lean, hollow-eyed, old, beetle-browed women are the most dangerous. "

1. Read Sources 9–11. List the reasons the writers give for there being more women witches than men.
2. On pages 20–25 you looked into the attitude of the Church to women in the Middle Ages. Are the attitudes of these writers similar to the attitudes to women in the Middle Ages?
3. Which of these 'reasons' could be used to explain each of the cases summarised in Sources 1–5?

Recent writers have suggested rather different explanations. Source 12 shows the ideas that have been put forward by modern historians.

SOURCE 12

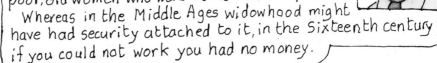

The changes in village life particularly affected women. Single, elderly women were more likely to be beggars than men, because men had more chance of getting work. It tended to be these poor, old women who were accused most often.
Whereas in the Middle Ages widowhood might have had security attached to it, in the sixteenth century if you could not work you had no money.

Some people accused of witchcraft were 'wise' or 'cunning' women.
In the Middle Ages there had been a wise woman or 'cunning' woman or man in each village. In the days before doctors these were people who had a genuine ability to heal the sick, using herbs and basic medical knowledge. They were thought to have special powers, but in the Middle Ages they were not brought to trial as witches. Usually they were valued or respected members of the village society.
However in times of anxiety about witchcraft people became worried about their special and strange powers. Wise women were liable to be accused of using black magic.

Some poor and powerless women, who believed in witchcraft, did curse people who had done them wrong. This was the only way they could get their own back in a society where everything was loaded against them. Whether you believe their curses were actually responsible for the things they were blamed for depends on whether you believed in witchcraft – in the sixteenth century most people did.

The Church and the State were run by men in the sixteenth and seventeenth centuries. Men also ran the witchcraft trials. Since most men believed that women were naturally weak and evil, they would assume that most witches were women.

4. Which of the ideas in Source 12 can be supported by Sources 9–11?
5. Which of the ideas can be supported by Sources 1–5?
6. With which of the ideas do you most agree ?

WHY WERE WOMEN ACCUSED OF BEING WITCHES?

Witchcraft trials

A witchcraft trial was a bizarre mix of different ingredients.

In some ways it was similar to a trial today. The accusers would be asked to present their charge. They would bring witnesses to support the charge. The accused would be asked to defend themselves.

However, once the witch craze really got going new elements were added, as you can see from Sources 13–19.

▶ **SOURCE 13** A late sixteenth-century picture of an Essex witch with her 'familiars'. These animals were supposed to suck blood from a mark on the witch's body. Before a trial the accused woman was examined for any suspicious marks. If a mark was found on the woman's body it was considered to be proof that she was a witch

▲**SOURCE 15** A witch is tortured to make him confess. Torture was forbidden in England but was allowed in Scotland

SOURCE 14 From a statement by John Wheeler in 1650 about the witch-hunts in the north of England

❝*The magistrates sent for a Scotch-man, who said he could find out witches by pricking them with pins, to come to Newcastle where he should try such who are brought to him. He would be paid twenty shillings a piece for all he should condemn as witches.*

When the sergeants brought the witch-finder on horseback to town the magistrates sent their bell-man through the town, crying, 'All people that would bring in any complaint against a woman as a witch they should be sent for and tried.'

Thirty women were brought in the town hall and stripped, and then openly had pins thrust into their bodies, and most of them were found guilty, near twenty-seven of them by him and set aside.

As soon as he had done and been paid he went into Northumberland to try women there where he got some three pounds a piece . . . if he had stayed in England he would have made most of the women of the north witches for money

[This witch-finder was later arrested and tried for villainy.]

On the gallows he confessed that he had caused the death of more than 220 women in England and Scotland all for the gain of twenty shillings a piece. He asked forgiveness and was hanged.❞

▲**SOURCE 16** This is the front page of an English pamphlet describing 'How to know whether a woman be a witch or not'. The illustration shows various moments in the story of Mother Sutton, who was said to be a witch

The Apprehension and confession of three notorious Witches.
Arreigned and by Iustice condemned and executed at Chelmesforde, in the Countye of Essex, the 5. day of Iulye, last past.

With themanner of their diuelish practices and keeping of their spirits, whose fourmes are heerein truelye proportioned.

SOURCE 19 An execution of witches in Chelmsford in the mid-sixteenth century

SOURCE 17 By a modern historian, Clive Holmes

At Lancaster Assizes in 1634 twenty people were convicted as witches. The accusation was supported by evidence of 'witch-marks'. Thirteen of the women were found to have marks – and these were located in the genital area.

The convictions troubled the authorities and they held up execution while four of the women were brought to London and re-examined.

. . . Pre-trial examinations of the accused by 'ancient skillful matrons and midwives' continued as a feature of witchcraft trials into the eighteenth century.

SOURCE 18 Written in 1631 by Friedrich von Spee, who had been a witch-examiner in Europe but later spoke out against the methods he had seen used

If she does not confess the torture is repeated – twice, thrice, four times. There is no limit.

If now under stress of pain she falsely declares herself guilty . . . she is also forced to condemn others, of whom she knows no ill, whose names are suggested to her by the examiner.

These in their turn are forced to condemn others, and these still others, and so it goes on: who can help seeing that it must go on without end?

1. List all the different methods that were used to prove that people were witches in Sources 13–18.
2. For each method say why it was unreliable.
3. Is there any evidence in the sources that people at the time thought these methods were unreliable?

How were witches punished?

Despite these methods of trial, witches were not always found guilty. If they were found guilty they were not always executed. The death penalty was usually only handed out if the witch was thought to have used her arts to kill someone.

Of 291 people accused of witchcraft at the Essex Assizes between 1560 and 1680, the majority (151) were found not guilty and the charges against them were dismissed. Of the remaining 140, 129 were found guilty. Seventy-four of these were executed and fifty-five imprisoned.

Imprisonment usually lasted a year, but the appalling state of prisons at the time meant that many died of 'gaol fever' before being released, or even before coming to trial.

In Scotland the situation was rather different. The Witchcraft Act of 1563 laid down a sentence of death by burning for anyone found to be a witch, or found to have helped a witch in any way.

Activity

Pamphlets were a popular way of spreading ideas in the seventeenth century.

Work in pairs. Make two pamphlets. One should be written by a witch-hunter, alerting people to the dangers of witches. Include an explanation why people should particularly beware of suspicious women.

The other pamphlet should be written by an opponent of the witch-hunts, telling people why they are wrong. Include an explanation of why women in particular are victims of the witch-hunts.

1. What do you think the witch trials tell us about:
a) the attitude of men towards women at this time?
b) the changing role of women?
Your teacher can give you an outline to help you answer this question.

Women try to be heard

DURING the seventeenth century lots of new ideas flourished. These included ideas put forward by women, and ideas about women as you can see from Sources 1–7.

> **SOURCE 1** In 1632 a group of women drafted a Resolution of Women's Rights complaining that
>
> *Women have no voyse in Parliament. They make no Laws. They consent to none. They cancel none. All women are understood either married (or about to be married) and their desires are therefore subject to their husband.*

In 1641, on the eve of the Civil War, Anne Stagg presented a petition to Parliament from 'Gentlewomen and Tradesmen wives'.

> **SOURCE 2** From the 1641 petition
>
> *[women's views should be heard by Parliament:]*
> *First because Christ died to save women as well as men.*
> *Second because the happiness of women as well as men comes from being free to follow Christ's laws, and having a strong Church and state.*
> *Third, because women share the calamities that happen when the Church or kingdom is oppressed.*

This first petition was welcomed by Parliament. However, when a second petition was put in a year later Parliament got the army to send the women away.

After the Civil War some women again presented a petition to Parliament calling for women to be involved in law-making. Source 3 shows the answer they received.

For some people the idea of women being involved in political life was so silly as to be laughable. For others there were real worries that this would be a dangerous change.

> **SOURCE 3** Parliament's reply to the Humble Petition 1649
>
> *The House gave an answer to your husbands. Go home and meddle with your housewifery.*
> *It is fitter for you to be washing your dishes. Things are brought to a fine pass if women teach Parliament how to make laws.*

SOURCE 4 A pamphlet called *The Parliament of Women* published in 1645

> **1.** Look at Source 4. Is this supporting or opposing women's demands?

The Ranters Ranting:

WITH

The apprehending, examinations, and confession of *Iohn Collins*, *I. Shakespear*, *Tho. Wiberton*, and five more which are to answer the next Sessions. And severall songs or catches, which were sung at their meetings. Also their several kinds of mirth, and dancing. Their blasphemous opinions, Their belief concerning heaven and hell. And the reason why one of the same opinion cut off the heads of his own mother and brother. Set forth for the further discovery of this ungodly crew.

Behold our joy to our Fellow-Creature.

Welcome Fellow-Creature.

Let us eat while they dance.

Decemb: 2   LONDON
Printed by B. Alsop, 1650.

◀ **SOURCE 5** An anti-Ranter pamphlet, published in 1650

2. Look at Source 5. Which of the Ranter activities shown do you think Parliament would be most worried about and why?

3. Most historians say that the women who presented petitions and wrote pamphlets were very untypical, and that there were only a few women who were actually active in these protests. Do you think that means that these protests were not very important? Explain your answer.

Pamphlets were another way that women could make themselves heard. Before the Civil War the government had censored books and pamphlets. After the Civil War censorship collapsed. Now any group could publish its ideas.

There were new religious groups which allowed women to be leaders. Some women wrote pamphlets spreading their ideas. In Source 6 a religious leader, Mary Cary, challenged the superiority of men.

SOURCE 6 Written by Mary Cary in 1645

“ *The time is coming when not only men but women shall prophesy; not only old men but young men; not only those who have university learning but those who have it not, even servants and handmaids.* ”

Opponents also published pamphlets such as Source 4 attacking these views.

In the 1650s the government stirred up a great fuss about a group called the Ranters. Nowadays some historians think that the government invented the Ranters to discredit all extreme groups. Source 5 shows some of the things they said the Ranters believed in and did.

Activity

It is 1675. You have read the statement by Hannah Wooley in Source 7.

SOURCE 7 Written by Hannah Wooley in 1675

“ *Most people in this age think a woman wise enough if she can tell her husband's bed from another's. Men tend to think we are merely intended to produce children, but if we had the same literature as the men they would find that our brains are as fruitful as our bodies.* ”

Work in pairs to make the front cover of a pamphlet to get across this message to Members of Parliament.

How did women's work change during the Industrial Revolution?

YOU are now going to move on to study the eighteenth and nineteenth centuries. In this period, women's lives underwent some major changes. Many historians argue that their status declined. As you work through these investigations, you can decide for yourself whether you agree.

The Industrial Revolution

From the Middle Ages until the seventeenth century the home had been the centre of work for both men and women. A married woman could therefore combine her various responsibilities. She could look after children and keep her home going at the same time as farming on the family farm, helping her husband in his business or doing paid work, such as spinning or cloth-making, at home.

This pattern for women's work continued well into the eighteenth century. Source 1 shows a family making cloth at home in the eighteenth century.

SOURCE 1 Two engravings made in the eighteenth century, showing cloth-making at home – beating the fibres and spinning them into thread

1. Look at Source 1.
a) What are the women doing?
b) What are the men doing?
c) What are the children doing?
2. Do you think these pictures give an accurate impression of what it was like to work at home?

SOURCE 2 The effects on women's work of the Industrial Revolution

Changes	Effects on women
■ Products such as beer or cloth were mass-produced in factories more quickly and more cheaply than they could be at home.	■ Home-based workers could not compete with the factories. Women could no longer earn a living by making these products at home. Either they lost the income they had earned from such work, or they had to go to work in a factory – often a long way from their homes.
■ In the past craftsmen had usually worked in workshops attached to the home. Their wives and daughters would help out at busy times. From the eighteenth century onwards, craftsmen began to work in special workshops away from the home.	■ Women would not help in their husbands' businesses if they had to look after children at home.
■ In the past most families had owned a few strips of farming land close to their homes. In the nineteenth century there was a sharp drop in the number of family farms. Many men left farming altogether to move to a town. Those that remained in farming usually worked for someone else, rather than having their own land.	■ Fewer women worked in farming. Those women who did work on farms usually worked long hours in agricultural 'gangs', under the control of a 'gangmaster', rather than helping their husbands. Such work was not at all suitable for a woman who had children to look after.

Changes

From the beginning of the eighteenth century onwards the Industrial Revolution began to change the way in which many people worked. The home was no longer the centre of work. This particularly affected women.

There was still plenty of work which could be done at home, but now it tended to be low-paid work, such as making clothes or hats. All the better-paid jobs that had been created by the Industrial Revolution had to be done away from the home.

Women therefore faced a difficult decision. They could move to where the work was – which was often impossible to combine with looking after a house and children – or they could stay at home and take whatever home-based work they could find, while they looked after the children and the house.

Some took the decision to go to where the work was.

Case study 1: Textile factories

Women made good workers in textile factories. They were thought to be better than men at very fiddly tasks, such as tying threads of cotton, because their fingers were smaller and more nimble. They tended to do what they were told, and did not complain about long hours and bad working conditions. Above all, they were cheaper, because women were not paid as much as men.

Today we might think this unfair, but at that time nobody really questioned whether it was right to pay men and women differently. Employers assumed that men worked harder than women. They also assumed that men had to earn enough money to support their families, while women were only working to top up the wages of their fathers or husbands.

Sources 3–12 give various viewpoints on what it was like to work in a factory in the nineteenth century.

> **SOURCE 3** From the novel *Helen Fleetwood* by Mrs Tonna, published in 1841. A girl is describing her impressions of her first day at work in a cotton mill
>
> *Frames on each side of the room walk up to one another, and then back again, with a huge wheel at the end of each, and a big man turning it with all his might, and a lot of children of all sizes keeping before the frame, going backwards and forwards, piecing and scavenging.*
>
> *Mr South said there was no sitting down; but nobody would even think of it. Move, move, everything moves. The wheels and the frames are always going.*

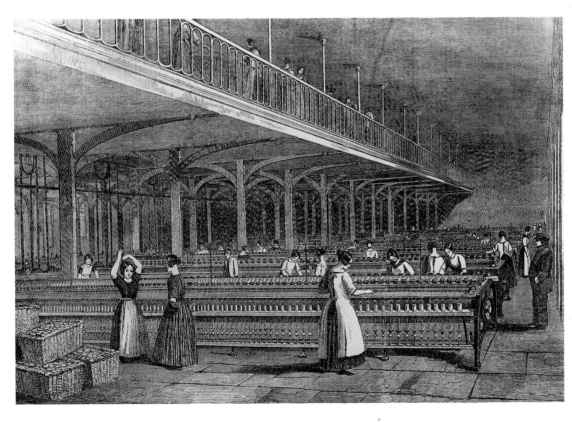

SOURCE 4 A nineteenth-century engraving of spinners in a textile mill

▶ **SOURCE 5** *Factory Workers in the Dinner Hour, Wigan*, painted in 1874 by Eyre Crowe

▼**SOURCE 6** Dinner time at a Manchester cotton factory, 1872, from the *London Graphic*, a weekly magazine

SOURCE 8 Written by a the historian, J.H. Murray, in 1982

Factory work for women was unskilled, monotonous, and unhealthy. Conditions in cotton mills resulted in a poisoning of the lungs from the dust, in pottery factories lead poisoning, in match factories phosphorous poisoning.

SOURCE 9 Written by a male factory inspector in 1884

The vast majority of the persons employed are females.

Their labour is cheaper, and they are more ready to undergo severe tiredness than men, either from the praiseworthy motive of supporting their families, or from the foolish of satisfying their love of nice clothes.

SOURCE 7 John Roebuck, a Member of Parliament, described a visit to a cotton mill in a letter to his wife, 19 June 1838

Amongst other things I saw a cotton mill – a sight that froze my blood. The place was full of women, young, all of them, some large with child, and obliged to stand twelve hours each day.

Their hours are from five in the morning to seven in the evening, two hours of that being for rest, so that they stand twelve clear hours. The heat was excessive in some of the rooms, the stink pestiferous, and in all an atmosphere of cotton dust.

I nearly fainted. The young women were all pale, sallow, thin yet generally fairly grown, all with bare feet – a strange sight to English eyes.

SOURCE 10 Lettice Bell, a nineteenth-century female writer, gave the following description of a factory girl coming out of work

There is no mistaking [the factory girl] in the streets. The long day's silence is made up for as soon as she is free, by loud laughter and a flow of language peculiar to her and her alone. No pavement ever seems quite wide enough for her requirements, as she strolls along from side to side, arm in arm with two kindred spirits.

SOURCE 11 Written by Clementina Black, an early trade unionist and campaigner for women's rights, in 1893

"*I must confess that if I were a mother of girls who had to choose between factory work and being a servant, I should give my voice unhesitatingly for the factory. The work would probably be harder, the comforts less, and the manners rougher, but the girls would be working among their own class and living in their own homes; and their health, their happiness, their friendships would be under their mother's eye.*"

▶ **SOURCE 12** A trade union card from the 1830s for the Power Loom Weavers' Society. In many parts of Britain women began to organise their own trade unions to improve their pay and working conditions

1. Compare Sources 5 and 6. Why do you think they give such different impressions of the factory workers' dinner hour?
2. Study all the sources. Using the sheet which your teacher will give you, draw up a chart to show the good things and the bad things about working in a textile factory.

Were working women a problem?

Work in textile factories was not the only industrial job done by women. Women also worked in coal mines, in potteries, in brickworks and in brewing.

The more women had to work outside the home, the more they were seen as a problem and a threat to society. Sources 13–15 explain what people seemed to be worried about.

SOURCE 13 Written in 1845 by F. Engels in *The Condition of the Working Classes in England*

"*The employment of the wife completely dissolves the family . . .*

A mother who has no time to trouble herself about her child, to perform the most ordinary services for it during its first year, who scarcely indeed sees it, can be no real mother to the child, and must inevitably grow indifferent to it, treat it unlovingly like a stranger.

The children who grow up under such conditions are utterly ruined for later family life, can never feel at home in the family which they themselves found."

SOURCE 14 From a speech by Lord Shaftesbury to the House of Commons on 7 June 1842

"*In the male the effects [of female employment] are very sad, but in the female they are far worse not only on themselves, but on their families, on society, and, I may add, on the country itself. It is bad enough if you corrupt the man, but if you corrupt the woman, you poison the waters of life at the very fountain.*"

SOURCE 15 In Elizabeth Gaskell's novel *Mary Barton*, one of the characters explains her objections to working women

"*They oughtn't to go to work after they're married, that I'm very clear about.*

I could reckon up nine men I know, who have been driven to the public-house by having wives who worked in factories; good folk, too, who thought there was no harm in putting their little ones out to nurse, and letting their houses go dirty, and their fires go out.

Was such a place tempting for a husband to stay in? He soon discovers gin-shops, where all is clean and bright, and where the fire blazes cheerily, and gives a man a welcome as it were."

1. Look at Sources 13–15. Make a list of reasons they give why women should not go out to work.
2. Do you think that any of these reasons would also apply to women working at home?

Lord Shaftesbury (see Source 14) was the most influential figure in the fight to limit women's work in factories and mines. He was appalled by the conditions in which women worked. But he was also appalled that married women should work outside the home at all (see Source 14). He came from a comfortable upper-class background. In upper- and middle-class families the women did not need jobs because they had plenty of money. Lord Shaftesbury and his supporters in Parliament applied the same principles to all women as they applied to middle-class women. Middle-class women did not need to work, so they stayed at home and looked after their children. Working-class women, said Lord Shaftesbury, should do the same. The result was a series of laws that gradually limited the work that women could do outside the home.

> **SOURCE 16** Acts of Parliament concerned with women's work
>
> **1842 Mines Act** Women are banned completely from working underground in the mines.
>
> **1844 Factory Act** Women are limited to twelve hours' work a day.
>
> **1847 Factory Act** Women are limited to ten hours' work a day in textile factories.
>
> **1867 Factory Act** Women are limited to ten hours' work a day in any place which employs more than fifty people.

The MPs who passed these laws said that they intended them to protect women from bad working conditions and bad influences, and to protect family life. However, when one looks closely at these laws one sees that their effect was also to limit women's opportunities. They could no longer work as equals with men in factories. The opinion of the government throughout the nineteenth century was that work outside the home was for men. Women should not have to work, but if they did they should be content to take lower-paid jobs and jobs that could be done in the home.

In most people's minds work was increasingly separated into women's work, which was low-paid, home-based work, and men's work, which was better-paid and away from the home. Source 18 shows you the kind of work women were doing in the 1870s.

> **SOURCE 17** Written by the modern historian Sally Alexander in *Women's Work in Nineteenth-Century London*
>
> *Only those sorts of work that coincided with a woman's natural sphere were to be encouraged.*
>
> *Such [laws] had little to do with the danger or unpleasantness of the work concerned. There was not much to choose between work in the mines and work in a London dressmaking workshop when it came to the risk to life or health. But no one suggested that sweated needlework should be prohibited to women.*

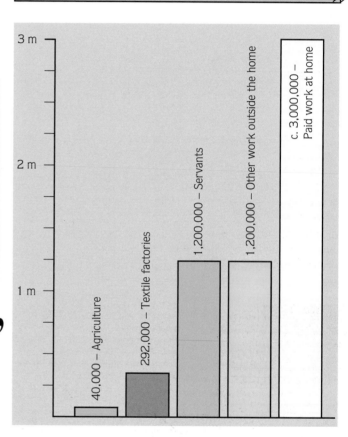

SOURCE 18 Women's employment in the 1870s and 1880s

> ### Activity
> You have been asked to write a speech for Lord Shaftesbury explaining why women should be discouraged from working. Use Sources 13–18 to help you. Include in the speech:
> a) what you think the role of women should be
> b) why you think it is wrong for them to work.

Case Study 2: Domestic service

You can see from Source 18 on the previous page that factory work was the exception rather than the rule for women. If a woman wanted a paid job it was much more likely that she would have to become a servant. Five times as many women worked as servants as worked in textile factories.

In 1750 there had been as many men servants as women, but men found they could earn higher wages and have greater freedom if they took up other occupations, such as factory work. By 1861 most servants were women and domestic service was regarded largely as 'women's work'.

You can see from the evidence on the next two pages that servants worked hard – probably harder than factory workers. But unlike factory work, domestic service was seen as a suitable job for women. It gave a disciplined environment and it took place within the house, so it was seen as 'ladylike'.

Some women worked 'in service' in the houses of the very rich, where there were many servants. Here, the servant had the advantage of being part of a little community. However, the chief servants, and in particular the housekeepers, were often very strict. Many girls went into service while they were still quite young. They started at the bottom of the servant hierarchy and could be badly bullied by those above them. They were made to work long hours at hard and dirty jobs, while the senior servants did the more skilled jobs.

SOURCE 19 In 1837 William Cother, a landowner in Gloucestershire, hired a new cook, Elizabeth Freeman, for £9 9s a year. He drew up this list of what he expected his new cook to do

66 *She says she can Cook, Roast and Boil Meat, Fry and Boil Fish, Make Pastry, Curry etc. etc.*
    Will obey orders without grumbling.
    Cut and leave Meat fit to come to table when cold.
Make no waste, leave no fat etc. etc.
    Use economy on all occasions.
    Ask leave whenever she goes from home.
    Never leave the House after night.
    Has no followers [boyfriends].
    Dinner sometimes to be got at short notice.
    Assist the other Servants on all occasions, particularly at Washing, Ironing etc.
    She is generally to go to Church every other Sunday morning.
    When she wishes to go to see her Friends (say once in three months) she might do so by asking two or three days previous. 99

1. Look at Source 20. Can you work out who is the chief servant (the housekeeper) and who are the most junior servants?

SOURCE 20 A photograph of the servants who worked at Easton Lodge, a large house near Dunmow in Essex, in about 1890

Other women worked in the houses of the middle classes. Many of these middle-class households could only afford one servant, a 'maid-of-all-work'. She would have to do all the jobs that in a larger household would be performed by a whole range of servants.

SOURCE 21 In 1860 Hannah Cullwick was employed in the house of Mr Jackson, an upholsterer from Kilburn in London. This is her diary entry for 14 July

I open'd the shutters and lit the kitchen fire – shook my sooty things in the dusthole and emptied the soot there, swept and dusted the rooms and the hall, laid the cloth and got breakfast – cleaned two pairs of boots – made the beds and emptied the slops, cleared and washed the breakfast things up – cleaned the silver – cleaned the knives and got dinner ready – cleared away, cleaned the kitchen – unpacked a hamper – took two chickens to Mrs Brewer's and brought a message back – made a tart and picked and gutted two ducks and roasted them – cleaned the steps and floor on my knees, polished the boot scraper at the front of the house – cleaned the pavement outside the house on my knees – had tea – cleared away – washed up – cleaned the pantry on my knees and scour'd the tables – scrubb'd the flags round the house and clean'd the window sills – got tea at nine for the master and Mrs Warwick – cleaned the privy and passage and scullery floor on my knees – washed the door and cleaned the sink down – put the supper ready.

SOURCE 22 From Mrs Beeton's *Book of Household Management*, 1861, a bestselling book on how a middle-class woman should run her house

The general servant, or maid-of-all-work, is perhaps the only one of her class deserving of commiseration: her life is a solitary one, and, in some places, her work is never done . . . The mistress's commands are the measure of the maid-of-all-work's duties.

SOURCE 24 Written by Harriet Martineau in an article on 'female industry' published in 1859

The doctor says that, on the female side of lunatic asylums, the largest class, but one, are maids-of-all-work (the other being governesses). The causes are obvious enough: want of sufficient sleep from late and early hours, continual fatigue and hurry, and, even more than these, anxiety about the future from the smallness of the wages. She has no prospect but to work till she drops, having from that moment no other prospect than the workhouse. With this thought chafing at her heart, and her brain confused by her rising at five, after going to bed at an hour or two past midnight, she may easily pass into the asylum some years before she need otherwise have entered the workhouse.

SOURCE 23 A maid-of-all-work, a photograph taken in 1880

◄ **SOURCE 25** An advertisement from *The London Graphic* magazine. What do you think the bells above the doorway are for?

▼**SOURCE 28** Maidservants photographed in the late nineteenth century. How old do you think the servants in this picture are? The photographer has posed this picture to show some of the jobs they might do in their daily work: washing, pastry making, peeling vegetables

SOURCE 26 Written by a nineteenth-century girl who worked as a servant

" *When a girl goes into service at a gentleman's house she is more liable to get into better company than factory girls. To be a servant is much more healthier and comfortable. Girls who are in service are generally much more quieter and more ladylike than those which are in a factory.* "

SOURCE 27 Written by a nineteenth-century girl who worked in a factory

" *When I was about fourteen years of age I went into service for about eighteen months and I did not like it at all because you are on from morning till night and you never get your meals in peace for you are up and down all the time. [In the factory] you have only got one to serve and you can go to as many classes in a week, you have got Saturday and Sunday to yourself and you can see a bit of life and are not shut up all day.* "

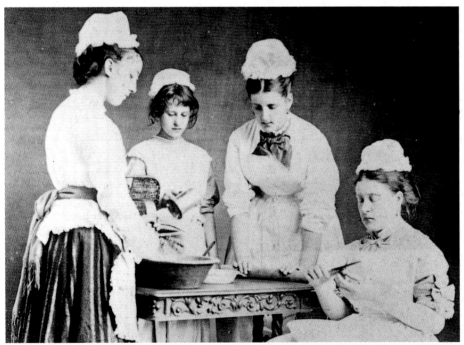

2. Source 21 describes a typical day for a maid-of-all-work. Draw a twenty-four-hour clockface, then fill in details of all the jobs Hannah Cullwick did during the day.
3. Can you see any evidence in Sources 21, 23 and 25 to support the view of maids-of-all-work given by Sources 22 and 24?
4. Would you rather have been a maid-of-all-work or a servant in a large house? Give your reasons.

Activity

Work in pairs. One of you has decided to take a job in domestic service, the other has decided to take a job in a factory. Each should write a letter to the other explaining why you have taken this decision. Use Sources 3–12 on pages 43–45 and Sources 19–28 to give you ideas.

Jobs for women

Most working-class women did not have a choice about whether or not they went to work. Women from working-class families had to work because their families needed the money to buy even the cheapest food and clothes. If they couldn't get factory work and they didn't want to work in domestic service there were many other jobs available, but the work was often very badly paid.

In the 'sweated' trades (see Sources 29–31) women worked in their homes or in small workshops for incredibly low wages, doing jobs such as sewing or making matchboxes or candles. At the start of the twentieth century a button-sewer in Birmingham could earn between eight pence and one shilling in an eighteen-hour day, if she sewed 2,880 buttons – but she had to pay for the cotton she used. Many women turned to prostitution. In London alone there were 200,000 prostitutes.

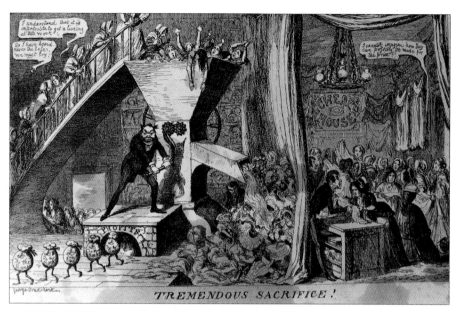

▲**SOURCE 29** A cartoon called *Tremendous Sacrifice* by George Cruikshank

▶ **SOURCE 31** 'Fisher-lassies' gutting fish at Stornoway in about 1900. The women lived in crowded lodgings and worked for very low wages

▲**SOURCE 30** A dressmakers' workroom, 1868

▲**SOURCE 32** Women field workers in Northumberland in about 1900

New opportunities

At the same time as women's opportunities in general were being limited, various 'female' professions began to appear.

Teaching

During the nineteenth century the population of Britain increased dramatically. The number of schools also increased. Education was made compulsory in 1870, so there was suddenly a massive need for new teachers. Many classes were taught by older children who had stayed on at school, usually girls. By the end of the nineteenth century three-quarters of all teachers were women.

Even so, the most powerful jobs in teaching (for example, as an inspector, visiting a school to check up on what it was doing) were almost always carried out by men. A headmistress would be paid the same as the youngest male teacher. Women teachers also had to be single. If they married they had to resign, whether they wanted to or not.

Nursing

During the nineteenth century many new hospitals were built. In 1860 the Nightingale School for Nurses was set up in London. By 1900, 60,000 trained nurses were working in British hospitals. British Voluntary Aid Detachment nurses won widespread praise for their work during the First World War. Nursing became almost invariably a woman's job, but nurses had to resign when they married.

Shop work

By the early 1900s the luckiest working-class girls were finding work in the new shops that were appearing everywhere. It was 'better-class' work, and the smartest London shops paid £1 a week, which was a good wage. But employees had to work an eighty-hour week, and they had to resign when they married.

Clerical work

In the early nineteenth century clerical jobs – writing up accounts in banks, writing letters, acting as secretaries, and so on – were done almost exclusively by men. In the 1870s the typewriter was invented, and male clerks were gradually replaced by less well-paid female typists. By the 1930s clerical work was regarded as a predominantly female occupation.

Most women office workers were from the middle class. The work was clean, 'ladylike' and not as tiring as teaching or nursing. However, male clerks were paid twice as much as women. Women also had to leave when they married.

Offices had separate entrances and stairways for women and some employers refused to let women leave the office at lunch-time.

SOURCE 33 Women office workers

Complicated changes

As you have seen, the Victorian period was a time of fairly complicated changes in the pattern of women's employment. By 1900:

■ Women were still involved in many areas of industry – but not in the heavier industries such as mining.

■ The majority of women worked as servants, in their own homes or in 'sweated' trades – work which was not controlled by government laws.

■ Opportunities opened up for educated women to work in the so-called 'white-collar' professions of teaching, medicine and clerical work, which were to become increasingly important in the twentieth century.

■ Women were still barred from many professions. They could not be lawyers or architects, or even serve on a jury.

■ In almost all jobs done by both men and women, women were still paid less than men.

Activity

Use pages 42–51 to fill out a chart like this:

Type of work				
How did it change in the nineteenth century?				
Was this a change for the better or the worse?				
Why?				

The angel in the house: the middle-class ideal?

IF WE are going to understand the changes in women's work in the nineteenth century, we must understand what a man's image of the ideal woman was at that time.

The expansion of industry in Britain and the growing wealth of many families increased the size of the middle classes and made them much more influential.

In middle-class households women were not expected to have a job. This was one of the things that marked them out as different from the working class. A middle-class man was expected to earn enough money to keep his wife and children in comfort. In return, the middle-class woman was expected to look after her husband and family.

This relationship between men and women was supported by special laws. When a woman married, all her possessions became her husband's property. Indeed, *she* became his property. He was not even committing a crime if he hit her.

Sources 1–6 show the kind of qualities that were expected of an 'ideal' wife in a middle-class home.

A Victorian husband saw the ideal wife as an 'angel in the house'. She was kind and loving, and gave up her own comfort for the sake of her husband or children. In return, she would be loved by those around her.

While the husband was expected to be strong and healthy, the 'angel' was seen, in contrast, as a weak creature. She was tender and delicate. Artists painted her with a sickly sort of beauty. She had pale skin and a thin, weak figure. Some writers suggested that she should also be rather foolish, and interested in only the most trivial matters. Others felt that she should have a certain amount of education, but only to make her a better wife and mother. However, they agreed that she should not try to take on a man's role.

SOURCE 1 George Elgar Hicks' painting, *Woman's Mission: Companion of Manhood*, 1863

1. Look at Source 1. What is the artist saying should be the role of a woman?
2. Look back at Source 12 on page 32 about Mary Queen of Scots. Does the information in this painting help explain why people in the nineteenth century were fascinated by her? Explain your answer.

SOURCE 2 Written in 1845 by Sarah Ellis

As a woman, the first thing of importance is to be content to be below men – below them in mental power, in the same proportion that you are in bodily strength.

► **SOURCE 3** *The Evening Hymn,* a nineteenth-century engraving illustrating a collection of short stories

SOURCE 4 The Victorian period saw magazines for women becoming very popular. *The Magazine of Domestic Economy* was started in 1835. It came out once a month. It cost sixpence and was aimed at middle-class women. This was its motto

66 We are born at home, we live at home, and we must die at home, so the comfort and economy of the home are of more deep, heartfelt, and personal interest to us, than the public affairs of all the nations in the world. 99

SOURCE 5 Written by John Ruskin in 1865 in *Sesame and Lilies*

66 The man's power is active, progressive, defensive. He is above all the doer, the creator, the discoverer, the defender. His mind is for thinking and invention; his energy is for adventure, for war, and for conquest, whether war is just, wherever conquest necessary.

The woman's power is not for battle, but for rule [within the home] – and her mind is not for invention or creation, but for sweet ordering, arrangement and decision . . .

She must be lastingly, incorruptibly good; unfailingly wise – wise, that is, not to improve herself, but to sacrifice herself: wise, not that she may set herself above her husband, but that she may never fall from his side. 99

The Victorian woman was also expected to be a good Christian and to pray regularly. For many women religion was a source of strength, as it helped them to bear the tragedies of life, such as the deaths of children and the pains and dangers of childbirth. But, on the other hand, the Church helped to reinforce the idea that wives were servants to their husbands and that they should sacrifice themselves for the sake of their family. Above all, religion seemed to support the view that women of the middle class should not get any pleasure out of sex. A popular manual for married women, *The Child: Its Origin and Development*, referred to sex as a 'sacrifice'. It was an 'ordeal' which married women were expected to go through.

3. Using Sources 1 to 5, make a list of qualities that nineteenth-century artists and writers thought an ideal wife should have.
You can get a chart from your teacher to help you answer questions 3–5.
4. Are they similar qualities to those which were valued in a wife in
a) medieval times (see page 15) or
b) the seventeenth century (see pages 27–29)?
5. Are they similar qualities to those which are valued today?
6. Use your answers to questions 3–5 to write your own essay on how the image of the ideal wife had changed over the period you have studied. You can get an outline from your teacher to help you.

An influential woman: the achievements of Josephine Butler

YOU MAY have the impression that Victorian women had little choice in how they lived and that most of them accepted their domestic role quite willingly. For many women, this was indeed the case – but not for all.

During the nineteenth century a significant number of women turned against the conventional female role and carved out independent lives for themselves. They became leaders in various spheres of life and greatly influenced the society around them. At the same time, they encouraged people to reconsider the position of women.

Source 1 shows some of them.

Marie Lloyd (1870–1922) was a very popular music-hall singer, who performed in Britain, America, Australia and South Africa

Florence Nightingale (1820–1910) Nursed in the Crimea, set up nurses' training schools in Britain and improved hospitals

Mary Seacole (1805–1881) Nursed in the Crimea and travelled in many countries

Annie Besant (1847–1933) was a campaigner for women's rights, birth control and socialism.

Mary Kingsley (1862–1900) travelled in West Africa and was an expert in local cultures.

Josephine Butler (1878–1906) was a campaigner for women's rights, birth control and socialism

Charlotte Brontë (1816–1855) wrote bestselling novels including Jane Eyre

Queen Victoria (1819–1901) was Queen of the United Kingdom and the British Empire.

SOURCE 1 Some of the influential women of the nineteenth century

Josephine Butler

Josephine Butler was born in 1828 at Dilston in Northumberland. Her father, John Grey, was involved in the anti-slavery campaigns. Her mother was very religious. Josephine also became very religious.

In 1852 she married George Butler, who worked at Oxford University. He too was a very religious man. Josephine Butler became the first woman to use the University Library when she worked as her husband's research assistant there. Their marriage seems to have been extremely happy.

> **SOURCE 2** From Josephine Butler's memoirs, written in 1892
>
> 66 *[In my husband George] the idea of justice to women, of equality between the sexes, seems to have been instinctive. He never needed convincing. He had his convictions already from the start – straight and clear.* 99

She did not have so high an opinion of her husband's colleagues. When they came round to her house and talked wittily and brilliantly together she says she 'sat silent, the only woman in the company, and listened, sometimes with a sore heart', because their opinions were at odds with those she held so deeply.

For example, in 1853 *Ruth*, a novel by Mrs Gaskell, was published. It was about a 'fallen woman' – an unmarried mother. The book provoked much discussion at the Butlers' house. The novel and its theme were condemned by the men.

This concern was to drive Josephine Butler into a campaign that she pursued through the rest of her life – helping prostitutes.

> **SOURCE 3** From Josephine Butler's memoirs
>
> 66 *A pure woman, they stressed, should be absolutely ignorant of certain evils in the world, even if those evils affected other women cruelly. One young man seriously declared that he would not allow his own mother to read such a book. Yet this was a book which seemed to me to have a very wholesome tendency, although dealing with a painful subject.* 99

SOURCE 4 A painting by Richard Redgrave called *The Outcast*, painted in 1851

> 1. Why do you think Josephine Butler kept silent in the discussion described above?
> 2. If she had decided to react to the man she mentions in Source 3, what do you think she might have said?
> 3. Source 4 is a popular picture from Victorian times called *The Outcast*. What do you think is the story behind this picture?

AN INFLUENTIAL WOMAN: THE ACHIEVEMENTS OF JOSEPHINE BUTLER

In 1864 Josephine Butler's five-year-old daughter was killed in a fall. After this tragedy Josephine and her husband moved to Liverpool with their two surviving children.

In Liverpool she started visiting the local prison. In the prison there were many prostitutes. Prostitution was a major industry in all British cities. It is estimated that there were 200,000 prostitutes in London. On average, a man visited a prostitute between one and seven times a week. Josephine Butler began a series of famous campaigns for better treatment for prostitutes and for refuges for poor and ill women to be set up.

Her most significant campaign was her fight against the **Contagious Diseases Acts** which were introduced in 1866 and 1869. Contagious, sexually-transmitted diseases, such as syphilis and gonorrhoea, were very common in the nineteenth century. They could be caught and passed on by both men and women and could be fatal.

They were particularly common in the army and navy.

Politicians were worried that the health and the morals of the nation were at risk. They passed laws that in 'garrison towns' (where there were many soldiers and sailors) any woman who was suspected of being a prostitute could be stopped and forced to undergo an examination to see if she had a sexually-transmitted disease.

If a prostitute did have a disease, she would be sent to a 'Lock Hospital' until she was cured. Whether she had a disease or not, she had to return for a repeat examination every twelve months. Anyone who refused to be examined faced imprisonment for up to three months.

Although these laws applied only to garrison towns, Parliament intended that they should soon be extended to the whole country.

Josephine Butler organised a campaign against these Acts.

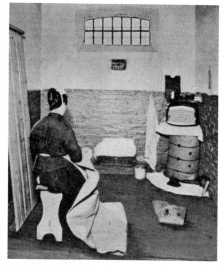

SOURCE 5 A prison cell c. 1900

At a time when most middle-class women were supposed to pretend to know nothing about sex, let alone prostitution, Butler made her campaign a public crusade. The Appeal (Source 6) was signed by 251 women, including well-known figures such as Florence Nightingale.

Josephine Butler was called to Parliament to explain her objections to the Acts.

SOURCE 6 Extracts from the *Ladies' Appeal and Protest Against the Contagious Diseases Act*, written by Josephine Butler in 1870

“
1 *Unlike all other laws for the repression of contagious diseases, these two laws apply to women only, men being wholly exempt from their penalties.*

2 *The law is supposed to be framed for [prostitutes]. But in order to reach these, all the women living in the districts where it is in force are brought under the provisions of the Acts. Any woman can be dragged into court, and required to prove that she is not a common prostitute.*

3 *We consider that arrest, forced surgical examination, and imprisonment with hard labour, to which these Acts subject women, are punishments of the most degrading kind.*

4 *By such a system, the path of evil is made more easy for our sons and for the whole of the youth of England . . . for in doing this the state declares that the vice [sleeping with prostitutes] is necessary and not very serious.*
”

Activity

Read Source 6. Imagine that you have been asked by Josephine Butler to make a wall poster publicising her criticisms of the Acts.

For each of the four points in Source 6, think of a headline which you could use on your poster.

SOURCE 6 From Josephine Butler's testimony to Parliament, May 1882

“*There is nothing in the physical being of man which matches the sacredness of the maternal functions in a woman, and these functions and every part of the body connected with them ought to be held in reverence by man . . .*

I am not here to represent virtuous women alone: I plead for the rights of the most virtuous and the most vicious equally, and I speak for the womanhood of the world. We are bound together in solidarity. You will find us so . . . Every woman has a right, a Divine right, to protect the secrets of her own body.”

Josephine set up the Anti-Contagious Diseases Acts Association, which published a weekly newspaper called *The Shield*. Sources 8 and 9 come from *The Shield*.

SOURCE 8 From *The Shield*, 7 May 1870. Butler is describing her visit to five women who were in Dover prison for refusing to undergo compulsory examinations

❝*I could tell them of the sympathy of women throughout the whole kingdom. In expressing this sympathy I never fail to let them feel how we hate the sin of their lives while we are indignant at the law which degrades them still further. But many I saw were not prostitutes.*❞

SOURCE 9 From *The Shield*, 14 May 1870. Butler is quoting the words of a prostitute she had interviewed

❝*It is men, men, only men, from the first to the last, that we have to do with! To please a man I did wrong at first, then I was flung about from man to man. Men police lay hands on us. By men we are examined, handled, doctored . . . In the hospital it is a man again who makes prayers and reads the Bible for us. We are had up before magistrates who are men, and we never get out of the hands of men till we die!*❞

Butler's campaign became very well known and she received support from many women. She held meetings during parliamentary elections at Colchester (1870) and Pontefract (1872), speaking against candidates who were supporters of the Acts.

She also had many opponents. Source 10 describes what happened one night in Pontefract.

SOURCE 10 From *Personal Reminiscences of a Great Crusade* (1896), by Josephine Butler

❝*We had to go all over the town before we found anyone bold enough to grant us a place to meet in. At last we found a large hay-loft on the outskirts of the town, We could only get up to it by a ladder through a trap-door. However, the place was large enough to hold a good meeting.*

We began our meeting with prayer. The women were listening to our words when a smell of burning was perceived, smoke began to curl up through the floor, and a threatening noise was heard below at the door. The bundles of straw beneath had been set on fire.

Then, to our horror, we saw appearing from the trap-door head after head of men with faces full of fury; man after man came in, until they crowded the place. There was no possible exit for us, the windows being too high above the ground, and we women were gathered into one end of the room like a flock of sheep surrounded by wolves.❞

Despite such opposition the campaign continued. The first success of Josephine Butler's campaign was that she managed to prevent Parliament extending the Acts to all parts of the country.

Then, in 1886, after sixteen years of campaigning, the Acts were repealed.

For the rest of her life, until her death in 1906, Josephine Butler campaigned for the cause of women, particularly in the field of education. For example, she successfully campaigned for universities and colleges for women to be set up.

1. Look back over Sources 2–10. Did Josephine Butler approve of prostitition?
2. Why did she want to help prostitutes?
Use evidence from Sources 2–10 to support your answers.

Activity
Using your own research, find out as much as you can about another 'influential' woman of the nineteenth century. You could choose one of the women in Source 1, or someone else who interests you.

Then use your research to write a profile of your subject covering:
a) her background
b) her activities
c) opposition she faced
d) whether she succeeded in her aims.
Draw a picture that illustrates one of your subject's achievements.

Activity
Look back at page 11. Repeat this same activity, only looking now at the way women are treated in textbooks about the nineteenth century.

Was it worth educating women?

DURING THE nineteenth century women campaigned for improvements to many aspects of their lives. One of the most successful campaigns was for better education.

In the Middle Ages the Church had been responsible for education, but it was not interested in educating women. In the sixteenth and seventeenth centuries, some non-Church schools were set up, but they, too, were only for boys.

However, in the seventeenth century it became increasingly fashionable for girls in richer or middle-class families to be taught to read and write by a tutor at home. Some received a much broader education as well. A few of these women went on to campaign for better education for all women (see Source 7 on page 41, for example).

> **SOURCE 1** Written by Mary Wollstonecraft in her *Vindication of the Rights of Women* 1792
>
> *I wish women to be educated not so that they can have power over men, but so that they can have power over themselves.*

> **SOURCE 2** An advertisement in *The Times*, London, 1843
>
> *Governess wanted. A lady belonging to the Church of England, competent to undertake the education of a young lady nearly sixteen years of age. She must be a person of cultivated mind, of great steadiness of character, sound good sense and cheerful temper. She is required to be proficient in the French, Italian and German languages, to be a good musician and capable of teaching the piano and singing well. A proficiency in drawing and watercolour is particularly to be desired.*

Activity
Look closely at Source 2. It shows what a middle-class girl's education usually consisted of. Plan out a possible timetable for a day's lessons.

By the early nineteenth century most middle-class girls received a basic education from a governess. However, girls from working-class families often received no education at all, and girls still could not go to university or college.

It was for these rights that women campaigned over the next 100 years.

Education for all girls
Only rich families could afford to employ a governess. However, in the early nineteenth century there were some schools for girls from poorer families:
- Sunday schools, run by churches. Children were taught to read the Bible
- factory schools for children who were working in a factory
- dame schools, which had to be paid for, and which were often no more than a child-minding service.

But most girls did not go to Sunday school, did not work in a factory and could not go to dame school because their parents could not afford to pay.

In 1870, however, there was a major change. The government made school compulsory for all boys and girls under ten years old. At first, these schools were not free, but cost a few pence per week per pupil. Many parents were unwilling to send their children to school, particularly when they could be working to earn money for the family. In rural areas attendance was very poor, particularly during busy times in the farming year, such as the harvest. Girls were absent from school three times as often as boys – particularly on wash-days or at harvest time. One headmistress wrote about this: 'I don't see how girls are to be prevented from helping their parents. But a boy ought never to miss an attendance unless there is not an elder girl in the family.'

In 1880, however, laws were introduced to force parents to send their children to school.

The schools taught all children reading, writing and arithmetic, but there were some subjects which were just for girls.

> **SOURCE 3** Written by a school inspector in 1874
>
> *A girl is not necessarily a better woman because she knows the heights of all the mountains in Europe, and can work a fraction in her head; but she is decidedly better fitted for the duties she will be called upon to perform if she knows how to wash and tend a child, cook simple food well and thoroughly clean a house.*

> **SOURCE 4** From the results of a survey carried out in 1899
>
> *After school a nine-year-old girl was at work on average for more than twenty hours per week, doing housework, baby-minding in other people's homes or helping her own mother.*

SOURCE 5 A photograph taken in 1908. What are the girls being taught?

1. What do Sources 3–6 suggest girls were being educated for?

SOURCE 6 Extracts from a school syllabus for girls introduced in Bristol in 1899

> *Housewifery*
> *Lesson 1: Laying a table. Preparing dinner.*
> *Lesson 2: How to light a fire. Cleaning kitchen flues and grates.*
> *Lesson 4: Bedrooms. Ventilation of room and bed. How to make a bed.*
> *Laundry work*
> *Lesson 1: Preparation for washing day. Rules for drying clothes.*
> *Lesson 7: Removing tea stains, fruit stains, etc. Washing and ironing table linen.*
> *Lesson 9: Washing, starching and ironing collars and cuffs.*
> *Cookery*
> *Lesson 1: Management of stove. Porridge-making.*
> *Lesson 4: Using scraps (remains of joint). Stock- and gravy-making. Boiling potatoes. Cocoa-making.*
> *Lesson 5: Dinners suitable for washing days.*

Going to university

If women were going to compete on equal terms with men, they needed to go to university. Almost all MPs, civil servants, doctors and lawyers had a university education. It was the passport to the best jobs or careers. Unless women were allowed into universities, such jobs would always be closed to them.

The campaign to get women into universities was a slow and gradual one.

1. Make a list of the ways in which girls' education changed in the nineteenth century, and the ways in which you feel it remained the same. Think about the following things:
   a) access to higher education
   b) how many girls were educated
   c) what women's education was intended for.

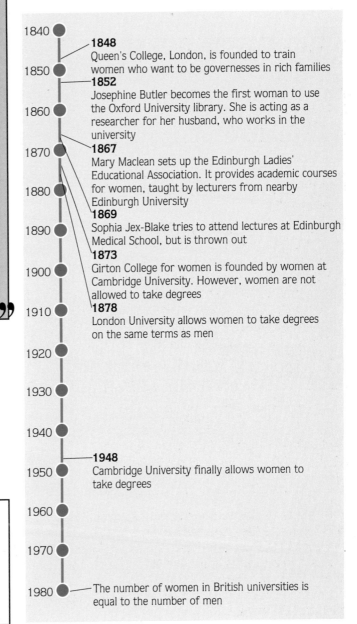

1848 Queen's College, London, is founded to train women who want to be governesses in rich families

1852 Josephine Butler becomes the first woman to use the Oxford University library. She is acting as a researcher for her husband, who works in the university

1867 Mary Maclean sets up the Edinburgh Ladies' Educational Association. It provides academic courses for women, taught by lecturers from nearby Edinburgh University

1869 Sophia Jex-Blake tries to attend lectures at Edinburgh Medical School, but is thrown out

1873 Girton College for women is founded by women at Cambridge University. However, women are not allowed to take degrees

1878 London University allows women to take degrees on the same terms as men

1948 Cambridge University finally allows women to take degrees

The number of women in British universities is equal to the number of men

The fight for women's rights

Caroline Norton

Caroline Norton was a bestselling novelist. She was married and had three sons. The marriage was not a good one. Her husband was a jealous and violent man, who often hit her. On a number of occasions she had to leave him and take refuge with her relatives.

In 1836 matters came to a head. Her husband took her to court. He accused her of having an affair with a leading member of the government. Although he lost the case, he then left her for good, taking the children with him, together with many of her possessions – including things given to Caroline by her family and things she had bought herself.

Caroline now discovered how far the law was biased against her. She had no right under law to see her children again. They were legally her husband's. Her husband was entitled to all her money and possessions – even the royalties she earned from her books. He even took the money that was left to her by her own father. When a newspaper libelled her, she discovered that she couldn't sue them herself because the courts did not recognise women. Legally, a husband had to sue on behalf of his wife!

She wanted a divorce, but the only way to achieve this was to take her case to the House of Lords and prove that her husband had committed bigamy or incest. This was an impossibly slow, expensive and degrading process for women. Not surprisingly, there had been only four successful petitions for divorce by women in 200 years.

---

1. Look back at page 15. How do Caroline Norton's legal rights compare with the legal rights of a woman in the Middle Ages?

For the next thirty years Caroline Norton led a vigorous campaign both to get justice for herself and also to change the laws that had left her helpless. She was well aware that she was not the only woman trapped in a bad marriage with no rights of her own. However, she was in a unique position in having both the writing skills and the contacts with influential people to mount a campaign against these injustices.

She wrote pamphlets and challenged leading politicians to reconsider the position of women. She wrote to Queen Victoria many times about both her personal situation and the general problems it exposed.

> **SOURCE 1** From Caroline Norton's letters to Queen Victoria
>
> " ■ *I have learned about the law respecting women, piecemeal, by suffering every one of its defects of protection.*
> ■ *I pray Your Majesty's attention to the effect of the married woman's non-existence in law . . . [my husband] has a right to everything I have in the world – and I have no claim on him.*
> ■ *From time immemorial changes in the laws of nations have been brought about by individual examples of oppression. Such examples cannot be unimportant, for they are, and ever will be, the little hinges on which the great doors of justice are made to turn.* "

Caroline Norton found that she had many allies among women, and even among men. Piece by piece, the wall of discrimination against women began to tumble.

The first breakthrough was in 1839, when women were given rights in regard to their children for the first time. The Custody of Infants Act gave mothers legal custody of children under seven years of age and rights of access to older children (provided that the mother had not committed adultery).

Gradual progress

By the 1840s Caroline Norton was only one of a number of women campaigning on two main issues:
- divorce – women wanted to be able to seek divorce on the same grounds as men
- property – women wanted the right to own their own property.

Was the nineteenth century a turning point for women?

Some historians regard the nineteenth century as a turning point for women. Others say that, even though laws were passed to improve women's status in society, in fact there were other developments that were a step backwards for women. What do you think?

Activity

You are a nineteenth-century woman campaigner. Choose one of the following tasks:

A. Write a letter to a newspaper complaining about how the status of women has declined during the nineteenth century.

B. Write a letter to a newspaper explaining how much has been achieved in the nineteenth century and that women have more rights than ever before.

You could get ideas about how to write your letter from Source 1. You could also look at page 12, which describes the position of women in the Middle Ages.

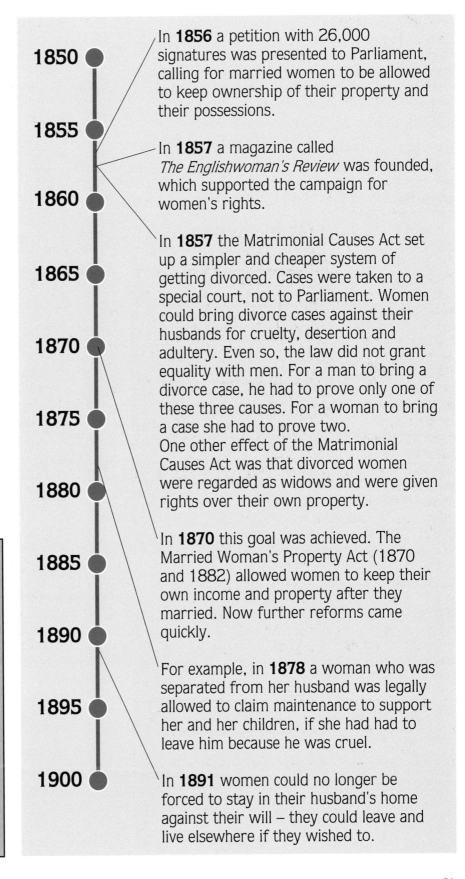

1850
1855
1860
1865
1870
1875
1880
1885
1890
1895
1900

In **1856** a petition with 26,000 signatures was presented to Parliament, calling for married women to be allowed to keep ownership of their property and their possessions.

In **1857** a magazine called *The Englishwoman's Review* was founded, which supported the campaign for women's rights.

In **1857** the Matrimonial Causes Act set up a simpler and cheaper system of getting divorced. Cases were taken to a special court, not to Parliament. Women could bring divorce cases against their husbands for cruelty, desertion and adultery. Even so, the law did not grant equality with men. For a man to bring a divorce case, he had to prove only one of these three causes. For a woman to bring a case she had to prove two.
One other effect of the Matrimonial Causes Act was that divorced women were regarded as widows and were given rights over their own property.

In **1870** this goal was achieved. The Married Woman's Property Act (1870 and 1882) allowed women to keep their own income and property after they married. Now further reforms came quickly.

For example, in **1878** a woman who was separated from her husband was legally allowed to claim maintenance to support her and her children, if she had had to leave him because he was cruel.

In **1891** women could no longer be forced to stay in their husband's home against their will – they could leave and live elsewhere if they wished to.

How did women win the vote?

By 1900 women had achieved many improvements in their education, legal rights and job opportunities. However, they could still not vote in General Elections. Many women believed that until they had this basic right to choose their own MP they would always be second-class citizens.

The NUWSS – the Suffragists

The campaign to win the vote for women began in the 1850s. By the 1870s it was a mass movement. Local groups held meetings all over the country to present the case for giving women the vote. There were 1,300 meetings in 1877–78 alone. The campaigners were mainly middle-class women. They were known as 'Suffragists'. ('Suffrage' means the right to vote.) In 1890 the hundreds of local groups from all over the country formed a national organisation (later named the NUWSS), led by Millicent Fawcett.

Millicent Fawcett and the NUWSS believed in peaceful methods of campaigning. Fawcett wrote in 1911 that she wanted the NUWSS 'to show the world how to gain reforms without violence, without killing people and blowing up buildings and doing the other silly things that men have done when they wanted the laws altered'.

SOURCE 2 A leaflet advertising the NUWSS pilgrimage to London in 1913

Sources 1–3 illustrate the tactics the NUWSS used instead. They issued leaflets, collected petitions and held meetings. They also met with politicians and argued their case. At election times they helped any candidate who supported women's suffrage.

By 1900 more than half of all MPs said they wished to give the vote to women. Millicent Fawcett said that her movement was 'like a glacier': it might be slow-moving, but it was powerful and unstoppable. She believed that in the end its tactics would get women the vote.

▼**SOURCE 1** The NUWSS pilgrimage arrives in London – a photograph taken in June 1913

> **SOURCE 3** Suffragist tactics, 1905–1910
>
> **1905** Run meetings in almost all constituencies in the run-up to the General Election.
> **1907** Hold their first procession.
> **1908** Lead a deputation to see the Prime Minister.
> **1909** Fawcett to hold a public debate with her opponents.
> **1910** Raise a petition of 280,000 signatures.

The WSPU – the Suffragettes

Some women lost patience with the tactics of the NUWSS. They said that the peaceful campaign was, in fact, getting nowhere. The newspapers seemed to take no notice of the campaign, so the public also ignored it. MPs had other things on their minds. While they might say at election times that they supported women's suffrage, whenever Parliament voted on the issue the vote was lost. (Women's suffrage was refused fifteen times up to 1900.)

In 1903 Emmeline Pankhurst and her daughters formed a breakaway group called the Women's Social and Political Union. They were nicknamed the 'Suffragettes'. Whereas the NUWSS had campaigned only for votes for women, the members of the WSPU also wanted to campaign for better working and living conditions for women.

Their motto was 'Deeds not Words'. Sylvia Pankhurst described their aims: 'To create an impression upon the public throughout the country, to set everyone talking about votes for women, to keep the subject in the press, to leave the government no peace from it.' Sources 4–6 show some of the things they did.

SOURCE 5 Mrs Pankhurst is arrested after a Suffragette demonstration outside the Houses of Parliament

> **SOURCE 6** Suffragette tactics, 1905–1910
>
> *1905 Heckling at meetings.*
> *1906 Deliberately try to get arrested and sent to prison – although they commit no violence themselves.*
> *1908 Start occasional attacks on property, such as breaking windows, etc.*
> *1909 Suffragettes in prison go on hunger strike. (Hunger-strikers are force-fed.)*
> *1912 Organise window smashing.*
> *1913 Carry out arson, bombing and sabotage in many areas of Britain.*

The WSPU's controversial campaigns won massive publicity for the women's suffrage movement. They were particularly successful in raising support in London. For example, there were thirty-four branches of the WSPU in London alone, but only fifty-four in the rest of the country combined. Half a million people attended their meeting in Hyde Park in London in June 1908.

> **SOURCE 4** A description by Emmeline Pankhurst of the Suffragettes' first public demonstration in 1905, at a meeting addressed by the Prime Minister and his Cabinet
>
> *At the end of the meeting, Annie Kenney, whom we had smuggled into the hall in disguise, called out in her clear, sweet voice: 'Will the Liberal Government give women the vote?'*
>
> *At the same moment, Theresa Billington let drop a huge banner with the words: 'Will the Liberal Government give justice to working women?'*
>
> *Just for a moment there was a gasping silence, the people waiting to see what the Cabinet Ministers would do. They did nothing. Then amid uproar and shouting, the women were seized and flung out of the hall.*

1. Use the information on this page to draw up lists of the similarities and differences between the WSPU and the NUWSS. Think about their aims and methods.

HOW DID WOMEN WIN THE VOTE?

Why had women not won the vote by 1914?

The Suffragettes' campaign was something totally new. When women took to the street to protest many men were shocked. They still expected women to be quiet and obedient. But the papers took notice, and suddenly the campaign for women's votes was important news.

Parliament was forced to debate the issue again and again. Each time it did, the Suffragettes mounted a demonstration. They were arrested, then refused to pay the fines, preferring to go to prison.

Once in prison, they went on hunger strike. Because the government thought a Suffragette who died would be seen as a martyr, they force-fed the hunger-strikers – a violent process which played into the hands of the Suffragettes. Posters such as Source 7 won them more sympathy.

Many people in Britain thought the police and government overreacted to the Suffragettes. Putting women in prison for three months for simply holding a meeting where it was not allowed, and then force-feeding them, seemed unnecessary. New members flooded into both the WSPU and the revitalised NUWSS.

Mrs Fawcett and the NUWSS did not approve of the Suffragettes' tactics, but they did admire their courage, as Sources and 10 and 11 show.

As the campaign for women's suffrage mounted, its opponents also became more organised, producing posters such as Source 8.

In 1911 it seemed as if the long years of waiting were over and that the women's campaign was about to succeed.

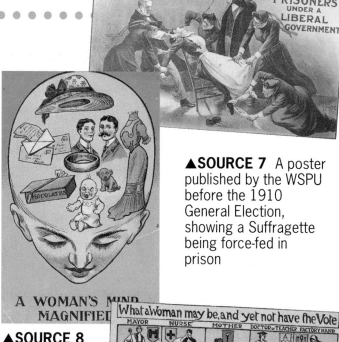

▲**SOURCE 7** A poster published by the WSPU before the 1910 General Election, showing a Suffragette being force-fed in prison

A WOMAN'S MIND MAGNIFIED

▲**SOURCE 8** An anti-Suffragist poster of 1910

▶ **SOURCE 9** A Suffragette poster of 1910

What a Woman may be, and yet not have the Vote
MAYOR NURSE MOTHER DOCTOR or TEACHER FACTORY HAND

What a Man may have been, & yet not lose the Vote
CONVICT LUNATIC Proprietor of white Slaves Unfit for service DRUNKARD

In May of that year Parliament gave a first reading to the Conciliation Bill, which would give women the vote. It had the support of all parties, and was passed by a massive majority of 167. The government announced that it would proceed with the Bill the following year.

Then, in November, the government changed its mind. It dropped the Conciliation Bill. Instead, it introduced a Franchise Bill, which didn't mention women, and said that Parliament could add women to this new bill if it wanted. When MPs tried to introduce women's suffrage to the Bill, they were told that this changed the nature of the Bill so much that it would have to be withdrawn.

The supporters of women's suffrage were incensed. Two hundred Suffragettes were arrested in scuffles with the police.

SOURCE 10 From a letter written by Mrs Fawcett to *The Times* when Suffragette leaders were in prison in 1906

❝ *I hope that the more old-fashioned Suffragists will stand by their comrades who in my opinion have done more [to advance the movement] in twelve months than I and my own followers have been able to do in the same number of years.* ❞

SOURCE 11 Written by Mrs Fawcett in 1911

❝ *The violence offered [by the Suffragettes] has not been formidable, and the fiercest of the Suffragettes have been far more ready to suffer pain than to inflict it.*

What those endured who underwent the hunger strike and the anguish of force-feeding can hardly be overestimated. Their courage made a deep impression on the public. ❞

SOURCE 12 Written by Mrs Fawcett in 1911

❝ *If it had been [Prime Minister Asquith's] object to enrage every woman Suffragist to the point of frenzy he could not have acted more appropriately.*

Years of unexampled effort and self-sacrifice had been spent by women to force upon the government the enfranchisement of women, and when the Prime Minister spoke the only promise he made was to give more votes to men. ❞

This setback triggered a wave of violence. The Suffragettes organised window-smashing across the whole of central London. Suffragette leaders, including Mrs Pankhurst, were imprisoned.

In prison they once again went on hunger strike. This time, instead of force-feeding the women, the government released them when they became very ill and close to death, then rearrested them as soon as they had recovered enough to return to prison. This became known as the 'Cat and Mouse Act', because the government was playing with the hunger-strikers like a cat plays with a mouse.

During 1913 Mrs Pankhurst went in and out of prison twelve times. Each time she was arrested she was frailer, and each time the Suffragettes reacted more violently and more angrily.

Moderate Suffragette leaders withdrew from the increasingly violent organisation and Mrs Pankhurst's daughter Christabel was left to run the Suffragette campaign from Paris. She helped plan arson and sabotage attacks throughout 1913.

It seemed to many people that the Suffragettes' campaign was out of control. When Prime Minister Asquith visited Dublin, an axe was thrown at him, missing him narrowly. Bombs were planted in railway stations and in Westminster Abbey. An explosion led to a fire at the home of David Lloyd George, the Chancellor of the Exchequer.

The violence played into the hands of the anti-Suffragists. Prime Minister Asquith was against women's suffrage, and the violence gave him a good excuse not to give in. He argued that if he gave in to such threats it would encourage other groups to do the same. The government knew that there were other groups, such as dockers and miners who were ready to strike for higher pay. Those people who wanted independence for Ireland, could also cause problems at this time.

The violence also turned many moderate MPs, who had previously supported women's suffrage, against it. When women's suffrage was debated in Parliament in 1913 it was defeated by forty-eight votes. Lloyd George said: 'Haven't the Suffragettes the sense to see that the very worst way of campaigning for the vote is to try to intimidate or blackmail a man into giving them what he would gladly give otherwise?'

The NUWSS worked hard to win back the support of the public, which the Suffragettes were losing. It encouraged poor working women to join by not making them pay a membership fee – over 50,000 more women had joined Mrs Fawcett's organisation by 1914. By the summer of 1914, however, the situation looked almost hopeless.

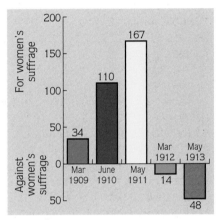

SOURCE 14 Votes on women's suffrage, 1909–1913

1. Say whether or not you agree with each of the following statements, supporting your answer with evidence from pages 62–65.
   ■ 'The Suffragettes' militant campaign was successful because it was the only thing that made the government pay attention to the demands of women.'
   ■ 'The Suffragettes' militant campaign of violence was a failure because it reduced support among the moderates and gave opponents an excuse to reject the idea of women's suffrage.'

2. Sources 10 and 11 give you Mrs Fawcett's opinion of the Suffragette campaign in 1906 and 1911. Write a paragraph to explain what you think she might have said in 1913 or 1914.

5 June
Purple dye poured into reservoirs near Bradford

18 June
Church in Rowley Regis set on fire

3 June
Boat-house in Oxford burnt down

31 May
Railway telegraph wires cut in Cardiff and Monmouth

9 June
Grandstand at Hurst Park racecourse in Surrey set on fire

30 June
Railway station at Leuchars junction set on fire

3 June
Acid poured onto the greens of a golf course near Doncaster

9 June
Cricket pavilion in Middlesex set on fire

2 June
Post-boxes in Lewisham set on fire

4 June
Emily Davison throws herself under the King's horse at the Derby horse-race

SOURCE 13 Suffragette activity in 1913

HOW DID WOMEN WIN THE VOTE?

The Great War

In August 1914 Britain declared war on Germany. Both the Suffragettes and the Suffragists suspended their campaigns. The leaders of the movements saw this both as a patriotic duty and also as an opportunity to assert women's rights by making themselves indispensable to 'the war effort'.

> **SOURCE 15** Written by Mrs Fawcett to members of the NUWSS in August 1914
>
> *Now is the time for effort and self-sacrifice by every one of us to help our country. Let us show ourselves worthy of citizenship, whether our claim to it be recognised or not.*

So many men had gone away to fight that women were needed to do their jobs. As a result, the number of women working in industry increased enormously.

The war made it acceptable for women to work in shipyards, collieries and brickyards, as they had done a century or more earlier. Some of them took on highly-skilled work as engineers, lathe-operators and carpenters. Later in the War, women made up most of the workforce in government munitions factories. In some of these jobs the women were welcomed. In others they were resented because, with little or no training, they did jobs which had previously been seen as being skilled.

Sources 16–25 tell you more about women's work during the War.

> **SOURCE 17** Written by Dr Butler, the government medical officer in a munitions factory in Scotland
>
> *There is no industrial work as heavy as charring [domestic service] and women should not be prevented from doing any work they are fit for, including foundry work, heavy engineering and heavy chemical work.*

> **SOURCE 18** Written by Sylvia Pankhurst
>
> *[The women] were painting aeroplane wings with dope varnish from 8 a.m. to 6.30 p.m.*
>
> *They were frequently expected to work on till 8 p.m. and were paid only bare time rates for this overtime.*
>
> *Meals were often taken in the horrid atmosphere of the workshop. It was common, they told me, for six or more of the thirty women dope painters to be lying ill on the stones outside the workshop for half an hour, or three-quarters, before they were able to return to their toil.*

SOURCE 19 A female tram driver

> **SOURCE 20** From a letter sent to the *Glasgow Herald* in 1916 by a women
>
> *To observe how men speak and write about women today is vastly amusing to us. We have not changed with the war; it is only that in some instances the scales have fallen from men's eyes . . . In the hour of Britain's need her sons have realised that if victory was to be won they could not afford to hem women in with the old restrictions . . .*

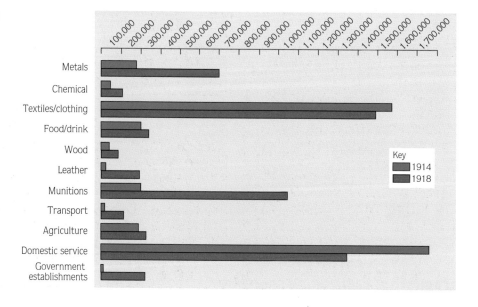

SOURCE 16 The employment of women in industry 1914–1918

SOURCE 21 Women making a lorry in an engineering workshop

▼**SOURCE 22**
A woman gravedigger

SOURCE 23 A comparison of the quality and output of women and men by the National Employers' Federation in 1918

❝Quality
Sheet metal – Women's work better than men's output
Aircraft woodwork – Women equal to men in most areas
Cartridge production – Women equal to men
Shell production – Women's work poorer than men's

Quantity
Sheet metal – Women's production equal to 99% of men's output
Aircraft woodwork – Women's production equal to men's output
Cartridge production – Women's production equal to men's output; in some cases 20% more than men's
Shell production – Women's production behind that of men and boys**❞**

SOURCE 24 Written by a modern historian, G. Griffiths, in *Women's Factory Work in World War I*, 1991

❝*Women working with explosives developed coughing, swellings and burns.*

During the first two years of the war, there were over 100 deaths from TNT [an explosive] poisoning, as well as many serious illnesses.

New sets of regulations on the safety and health of munitions workers included rules about cleanliness, ventilation, washing facilities, providing free milk, special uniforms and appointing full-time medical officers.❞

SOURCE 25 From a government report in 1919 on how effectively women had been brought into industrial work

❝*In every industrial district without exception there was continuous opposition [from men] to the introduction of women. In some cases this opposition was overt to the point of striking; in other instances . . . it took the insidious form of refusal to instruct women, or attempts to restrict the scope of their work or to discredit their efforts.*❞

Activity

Use Sources 16–25 to write a short report for a newspaper about women's war work in Britain.
Your report should include the following:
a) the kinds of jobs women are doing
b) how this is different from before the War
c) what conditions are like for women in various jobs
d) how men have reacted
e) what conclusions you draw about the way this is changing the role of women.

Why did women get the vote in 1918?

In 1915 the government realised it had a problem. The old voting system demanded that voters live in the same place for the twelve months before an election. So if there were to be an election during the War, most soldiers would not be able to vote. The government decided to change the law and make sure the 'war heroes' got their vote. Women's groups saw their opportunity and began to put pressure on the government to include votes for women in the changed law (see Source 26).

There were no demonstrations, but there were many meetings between women's leaders and politicians, and a flood of telegrams and letters were sent to MPs.

In 1918 Parliament finally passed a new law which gave all women over thirty the right to vote. After all the frustrations and turmoil of the pre-war campaign the women had succeeded in their aims. Why had the MPs changed their minds?

▼**SOURCE 26** A cartoon from the cover of *Votes for Women* magazine, 26 November 1915

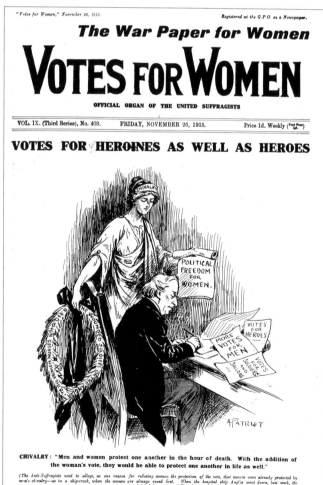

"Votes for Women," November 26, 1915. Registered at the G.P.O. as a Newspaper.

The War Paper for Women
VOTES FOR WOMEN
OFFICIAL ORGAN OF THE UNITED SUFFRAGISTS

VOL. IX. (Third Series), No. 403.　FRIDAY, NOVEMBER 26, 1915.　Price 1d. Weekly (Post Free 1½d.)

VOTES FOR HEROINES AS WELL AS HEROES

CHIVALRY : "Men and women protect one another in the hour of death. With the addition of the woman's vote, they would be able to protect one another in life as well."

(The Anti-Suffragists used to allege, as one reason for refusing women the protection of the vote, that women were already protected by men's chivalry—as in a shipwreck, when the women are always saved first. When the hospital ship Anglia went down, last week, the women nurses refused life belts, saying, "Wounded men first.")

SOURCE 27 Written by E.S. Montague, Minister of Munitions, in 1916

Women of every station . . . have proved themselves able to undertake work that before the War was regarded as solely the province of men . . . Where is the man now who would deny to women the civil rights which she has earned by her hard work?

SOURCE 28 Written by Sylvia Pankhurst in 1931

People's memory of militancy, and the certainty that it would return if the claims of the women were set aside, was a much stronger factor in overcoming the reluctance of those who would again have postponed giving women the vote.

SOURCE 29 Written by the historians D. Condell and J. Liddiard in 1987

By 1918 the Victorian image of womanhood – physically frail, sheltered, leisured, private – had been undermined by the wartime experience of both sexes. It was now permissible for women to be physically courageous, responsible, conscientious, cheerful and outgoing.

They assumed responsibility, endured physical hardship, mastered control of new technology, were financially independent through reasonable wages and obtained the right to join trade unions.

Many women had witnessed the suffering and anguish of men as they had not in previous wars, and had also worked side by side with men as comrades and friends. It was inevitable that this would start to change mutual perceptions, and the granting of the vote at last [to women over thirty] seemed entirely appropriate.

SOURCE 30 Written by modern historian Martin Pugh

The women who did most of the war work were young, single and working class. The politicians had no intention of letting them dominate politics. The government saw them as unstable, too much of an unknown quantity. They were much happier with the older married family women who had done less in the War and were not after jobs in industry – and who would probably vote exactly as their husbands did. It was these women who got the vote in 1918.

VOTE WON!

Commons Enfranchise 6,000,000 Women Over 30.

HUGE MAJORITY.

The Commons last night gave the vote to 6,000,000 women over the age of 30.

The proposal was carried by an overwhelming majority, the figures being received with loud cheers :—

For 385
Against 55
_____
Majority 330

The "antis" made a stubborn stand; but there never seemed any doubt as to how the debate would end, though the majority proved surprisingly big.

SOURCE 31 Part of the obituary for Mrs Fawcett, founder and leader of the NUWSS, from the *Guardian* newspaper, 6 August 1929

There were three stages in the emancipation of women:

The first was the long campaign of propaganda and organisation at the centre of which, patient, unwearying, and always hopeful, stood Dame Millicent Fawcett.

The second was the campaign of the militants [the Suffragettes].

The third was war.

Had there been no militancy and no war, the emancipation would have come, although more slowly. But without the faithful preparation of the ground over many years by Dame Millicent Fawcett and her colleagues, neither militancy nor the War could have produced the crop.

◀ **SOURCE 32** A headline from the *Daily Sketch*. Many newspapers who had criticised the suffragettes before the war switched to support them during the war

Activity

This diagram summarises some of the many reasons why women won the vote in 1918.

1. Make your own copy of the diagram.
2. From the sources on pages 62–69, find other reasons for their success and add them to the diagram.
3. Do you agree with Source 31? Explain your answer.

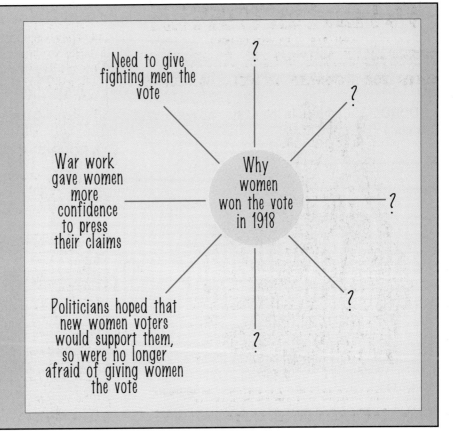

Need to give fighting men the vote

?

?

War work gave women more confidence to press their claims

Why women won the vote in 1918

?

Politicians hoped that new women voters would support them, so were no longer afraid of giving women the vote

?

?

?

Did getting the vote change anything?

CAMPAIGNERS such as Millicent Fawcett did not see getting the vote as an end in itself. They expected the vote to bring about wider social changes and improvements in the position and status of women. We are going to look at the areas of politics and work to see what happened in the 1920s and 1930s.

Politics

Before the War many men had feared that women would take over Parliament if they got the vote. This did not happen. In the 1918 elections only seventeen women stood as candidates, and only two were elected. Opponents of women's suffrage began to change their minds. In 1928 Parliament gave all adult women over twenty-one the vote by a majority of 387 to ten. This meant that women voted on the same terms as men. Now they really did form a majority of the electorate – 52.7 per cent. Yet in 1931 the number of women candidates was still only sixty-seven, of whom fifteen won a seat in Parliament.

Although men still dominated Parliament and political life, during the 1920s Parliament passed a series of reforms which would greatly affect women's lives (see Source 1).

were expected to give up their War work. Women who tried to hold on to their jobs were criticised by men and even, in some cases, physically attacked.

Some politicians argued that women who kept their jobs, and who were paid less than a man would be paid, were depriving men of jobs. Some even blamed the heavy unemployment of the 1920s and 1930s on women workers.

Women were expected to return to looking after homes and children, or to do traditional 'women's work' as servants or dressmakers, or other low-paid jobs. In place of the wartime advertisements urging women to 'do their bit' for the War effort, newspaper reports now urged women to go home and have more children (see Sources 2–4).

> **SOURCE 2** From the *Southampton Times*, 1919
>
> " *Women still have not brought themselves to realise that factory work, with the money paid for it, will not be possible again. Women who left domestic service to enter the factory are now required to return to their pots and pans.* "

1918	**1919**	**1923**	**1925**	**1929**	**1930**
First woman MP elected	Sex Disqualification (Removal) Act. Women could no longer be barred from any job because of their sex. The aim of the Act was to open up the professions. Women could now become lawyers, magistrates, architects, etc. It had little effect on jobs in industry. The law only applied to single women. A woman could still lose her job if she married	Women granted equal rights to men in divorce cases	The Civil Service admits women to government service for the first time. Women given the same legal rights over their children as men have always had	Margaret Bondfield becomes the first woman Cabinet Minister	The Government agrees to make contraceptive advice available to women for the first time. Women are now able to decide whether to have children or not

1918 1919 1920 1921 1922 1923 1924 1925 1926 1927 1928 1929 1930

▲**SOURCE 1** Changes in the rights and position of women, 1918–1930

Activity

Choose which of the reforms listed in Source 1 might seem most important to:
a) Josephine Butler (see pages 55–57)
b) Millicent Fawcett (see pages 62–69)

Work

During the War many women had done 'men's jobs' and had shown that they could do them just as well as men. Many of these women wished to stay in these jobs after the War. When asked, 'Do you wish to return to your former work or stay in the job you are doing now?', 2,500 out of 3,000 women said, 'Stay in the work I am doing now'. However, as soon as the War ended women

▼**SOURCE 3** Women's work in 1914 and 1931

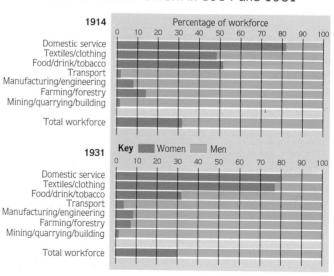

1914

Percentage of workforce
0 10 20 30 40 50 60 70 80 90 100

Domestic service
Textiles/clothing
Food/drink/tobacco
Transport
Manufacturing/engineering
Farming/forestry
Mining/quarrying/building

Total workforce

1931

Key Women Men

0 10 20 30 40 50 60 70 80 90 100

Domestic service
Textiles/clothing
Food/drink/tobacco
Transport
Manufacturing/engineering
Farming/forestry
Mining/quarrying/building

Total workforce

Most women did not want to return to the badly-paid jobs of the pre-war period. Their new jobs gave them more money, greater freedom and an improved status in society. But they had no choice. By the 1930s women were doing much the same as they had been before the War.

■ Women's wages were only half those of men, even if they were doing the same work.

■ Many trade unions continued to oppose greater working opportunities for women because they were a threat to men's jobs and wages.

■ Only a minority of working women belonged to trade unions, so they did not organise themselves to fight for better pay and working conditions.

▲**SOURCE 5** In 1930 Amy Johnson became the first woman to fly solo to Australia. The flight took eighteen days and included an emergency landing in the Iraqi desert. Her courage and independence were widely praised

> **SOURCE 4** From a report by R.E. Graves, Chief Inspector of Factories, in 1919
>
> 66 *The first year after the end of the War has been a very important one for industry. It is remarkable how complete has been the changeover from war to peacetime production. The first great step in the transformation was the gradual and now almost complete withdrawal of women from the men's industries.* 99

> **1.** Study Sources 1–4. Did getting the vote do anything to secure women's equality at work in the 1920s and 1930s?

Other changes

However, the 1920s and 1930s brought about other kinds of change:

■ Better advice about contraception meant women could choose to have fewer children.

■ Young women no longer had chaperones. They were able to go to the cinema or to dances with boyfriends without having to take an aunt or a female friend along.

■ Women's clothing became much simpler and less restrictive.

■ Make-up became acceptable.

■ Some women even dared to wear one-piece swimming costumes, instead of the pre-War costumes with sleeves and skirts.

The War had also given many women greater confidence. There were more and more successful women whose stories were reported in the newspapers and whom other women could look to as rolemodels.

SOURCE 6 Clothes worn by young women in 1905 and 1935

> ### Activity
> 1. Choose one of the changes listed below and explain why it might improve the lives of women, and what kind of women might benefit the most:
>   ■ better advice about contraception
>   ■ simple fashions
>   ■ women being able to fly aeroplanes
>   ■ girls not needing to have chaperones.
> 2. Choose the change that you think is the most significant and explain your choice.
> 3. Do you think any of these changes would have happened if women had not been given the vote? Explain your answer.

Have women won equal rights with men in the twentieth century?

How do we find out about twentieth-century women?

When you studied women in the Middle Ages you found out how little evidence there was about the lives of ordinary people.

When you studied the sixteenth and seventeenth centuries you found there was more evidence available from people's private lives than there had been from the Middle Ages. However, we still knew more about rich and powerful women than about ordinary women.

There is a big change, however, when we study the nineteenth and twentieth centuries. We have a lot more evidence about women's lives, and it tells us about a much wider range of people.

Activity

Work in pairs to fill out a table like this:

Evidence	How it helps us find out about women's lives	Available from the Middle Ages? or the sixteenth and seventeenth centuries

1. Look through pages 42–71. In the first column list all the different kinds of source used to find out about women's lives in the nineteenth and early twentieth centuries.
2. In the second column write what aspect of women's lives it helps you find out about.
3. In the third column say whether or not the same kind of evidence about women survives from the Middle Ages or the sixteenth and seventeenth centuries.
4. Choose the most useful new kind of evidence (ie evidence that was *not* available for the earlier periods) and explain why it is particularly useful.

Oral history

In this study of the changing role of women we are now moving on to more recent history from the 1940s to the present day. This has been a period of great change for many women.

This is also a period that is within the living memory of many people alive today. Your parents and grandparents lived through the changes we are going to investigate.

One of the best ways, therefore, to find out about these changes is to talk to people about them. This is called 'oral history', and it is one really valuable way of finding out about the recent past.

You are going to use your own oral history research to find out about two different topics:
- how women's lives were affected by the Second World War, and
- how women's lives were affected by the women's rights movements of the 1960s and 1970s.

Read the background about these two periods, then try out the 'oral history' activity on page 76.

SOURCE 1 Women and their families shelter in a London Underground station

Background: The Second World War

During the Second World War (1939–1945) women were expected to fulfil many of the same duties and roles as they did in the First World War (see pages 66–67). Once again they were called upon to work in industry, on farms, as nurses and in the forces – although not in the front line.

There were important differences, however.

■ In 1941 every woman had to register for War work. Many more women were involved than in the First World War.

■ In the First World War civilian casualties were very low. In the Second World War the War came to the towns and cities of Britain, with nightly bombing raids by German aircraft. Women were now in the 'front line' of attack in a way they had not been in the First World War.

■ Other changes, such as the evacuation of children and strict food rationing, greatly affected every woman's life in Britain.

■ In the First World War the trade unions had largely resented and resisted women taking men's jobs. In the Second World War the male-dominated trade unions agreed that women had equal rights to employment.

Even so, when the War ended there was a sense of history repeating itself. Women were once again demoted when the men came back and married women were asked to return to their homes as the following 'oral history' interview shows:

> **SOURCE 2** From an interview with a Leeds bank worker
>
> 66 *When all the men came back after the War the bank said, 'Thank you very much for doing all the work for our men while they've been away, but we are not going to have ladies on the counter. Now you've got to teach the men.' Instead of having four of us on the counter, they had seven men. We went back to the jolly old machines . . . the shorthand and the typing . . . we didn't get paid extra for teaching the men.* 99

Background: The women's rights movement

The 1960s was a boom time for some parts of British industry. Men's and women's wages were rising quickly, unemployment was not a major problem and many women had more money than ever before. The Prime Minister told the young people of the 1960s: 'You've never had it so good.'

In the 1960s the first effective contraceptive pill was made available to women. For the first time women could reliably decide whether and when to have children. They could therefore plan their careers more systematically, and in their relationships with men the Pill gave women a greater sense of freedom and equality.

Old ideas were being challenged in many areas of life. Television, which had first become available in the 1940s – but was bought only by the very rich – was present in the majority of homes in Britain by the 1960s. Television helped to spread ideas much more quickly than ever before.

In the 1960s more women than ever before went to university. With equal educational prospects, many women were becoming increasingly frustrated that the best jobs were still closed to them.

The result of all these pressures was that women joined together to form an active and often angry 'women's liberation movement'. Many things that had gone unquestioned for hundreds of years now came under attack.

The pressure was such that in 1970, for the first time, it became illegal to pay women less than men for the same work. In 1975 the Sex Discrimination Act outlawed discrimination in jobs, housing and other areas. In the longer term the movement gave women confidence to assert their rights in many areas, including their private lives.

The movement was not popular with many men, or with all women. 'Women's lib' was the butt of many comedians' jokes. Some also saw the movement as dangerously undermining the family. The same arguments that had been used against women working in factories in the 1830s were still being used in the 1980s.

> **SOURCE 3** From an interview with a woman who was born in 1949
>
> 66 *I wasn't prepared to just sit back and accept the role that my mother had. She was clever but had not had the chance to get a decent job because she'd spent all her time looking after kids. I wanted a good job, and it was good to be surrounded by women who felt the same.* 99

HAVE WOMEN WON EQUAL RIGHTS WITH MEN IN THE TWENTIETH CENTURY?

Activity

You are going to use oral history to see how these changes affected ordinary women. We can use oral history to find out about things that are not always written down, such as how women felt about their work and their family, or how they saw their position in society.

Stage 1 Work in pairs

Prepare a list of questions that could be used to interview a woman in her sixties or seventies about her life in the Second World War, OR a woman in her forties or fifties about her life in the 1960s and 1970s.

Think about:

home life —— where she lived
         —— who she lived with

work —— did she have a paid job? if so, what was it?
     —— at what age did she start work?
     —— did her mother work?

social life —— how often did she go out?
           —— where did she go?
           —— who did she go with?

Try to ask some questions to find out
a) whether the person enjoyed equal rights with men at home and at work, and
b) whether she felt she had equal rights. For example:
   ■ Were you paid as much as men doing a similar job?
   ■ Did you enjoy your job?
   ■ Did you feel your work was important?
   ■ Were there many jobs available to women?
If the woman has been married you could ask:
   ■ Did you feel your job was as important as your husband's? How did he feel?
   ■ Who did the housework?
   ■ Did you stop work when you got married or when you had children? If so, how did you feel about it?

If the person you interview has come to Britain from another country, you could ask about her experiences of British society, and how it compared with life in her country of origin.

Be prepared to make your questions appropriate for the person you are interviewing. If a woman has not been married, there is no point in asking questions about her relationship with her husband or her mother-in-law. If a woman has not had children,

there is no point in asking about the arrangements for maternity leave. Above all, the questions should be used as a way of encouraging the interviewee to tell **her own story in her own words**.

Stage 2 Find someone to interview

If you can think of a family friend or relative who would be prepared to answer some of your questions, that would be ideal. You can work in pairs, with one asking the questions and one taking notes, or you could use a tape recorder to record the interview and write it up afterwards.

Stage 3 Present your findings

Your class could put its findings together to make a wall display. You could present your oral history like this.

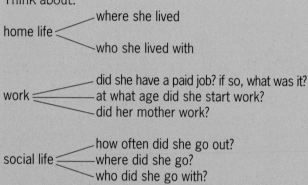

When I was eighteen I used to go to dances at the youth club, but I was never allowed to stay out after ten o'clock. My father was a policeman and he used to stand outside the hall in his policeman's uniform. If I wasn't out by five minutes to ten he would come in and get me, in front of all my friends. It was so embarrassing.

A woman in her fifties

I was working as a bank clerk in the 1950s, but when I got married I lost my job. It was company policy. They gave me some money, and I had to go. All married women had to go.

A woman in her sixties

One of the main reasons why I got married was to get away from home. There was no other way to do it in those days, you see. When I got married I had my own house and I could be more independent. Before that I just had to do what my mother told me. I couldn't go out or anything unless she said I could.

A woman in her sixties

You might be able to find some old photographs to illustrate the results of your interviews, and you could draw a map to show where all the people lived. You could then use your display, and the information from your interviews, to make a list of ways in which women's lives have changed, and ways in which they have stayed the same, covering areas such as work, social life and family life.

Have women won equal rights with men?

The battle for women's rights has largely been won.

In 1979 Margaret Thatcher was elected Prime Minister of Britain. Never before had a woman held this highest political position. Just a few decades earlier it would still have been unthinkable. When she took office Margaret Thatcher declared that 'The battle for women's rights has been largely won'.

Do you agree with her? Look at the evidence in Sources 4–13 and then decide.

SOURCE 4 Written by the historian Pat Thane in 1988

A gradually wider range of jobs has opened up to more [women], beginning with secretarial, clerical and teaching jobs at the end of the nineteenth century; more recently those giving access to real power – in the law, in banking, the civil service, as Prime Minister – for a very few, but still in numbers never known before.

SOURCE 5 From *Britain 1991*, a report containing information gathered by the government

1970 Women's average earnings were half of men's.
1970 Equal pay legislation was introduced.
1989 Women's average earnings were three quarters of men's.

Women's wages remain low partly because women tend to work in low-paid sectors of the economy, and because they work fewer hours than men.

SOURCE 6 From an interview with a representative of the Law Society on Radio 5 in April 1995

Fifty per cent of people entering the profession are women. Twenty-five to thirty per cent of people practising as solicitors are women. Yet in a big City law firm, with hundreds of partners, only half a dozen will be women.

Women tend to get pushed into doing matrimonial work (divorce, etc.) while men take other work.

Women are assumed just to be doing the job to fill their time before they go off to have a family.

From the **FIRST** domestic washing machine, launched in 1945, to the **IMPRESSIVE** new Activa range, Candy has been at the **FOREFRONT** of the appliance market throughout its 50-year history:

WASH in style

SOURCE 7 An advertisement from a women's magazine, 1995

SOURCE 8 A leaflet published by the Low Pay Unit

The Worst Paid Jobs in Britain 1995.[1]

According to the *New Earnings Survey 1995*, there are ninety-one occupations which pay below the Council of Europe's decency threshold currently £228.54 a week. From the ninety-one, twenty-four male occupations and seventy-eight female occupations appear below it.

Occupation	Average gross weekly pay	Sex
Petrol pump forecourt attendants	138.70	Female
Waitresses	140.40	Female
Kitchen porters, hands	142.90	Female
Bar staff	146.20	Female
Hairdressers, barbers	146.90	Female
Childcare assistant	148.90	Female
Shelf fillers	151.20	Female
Counterhands, catering assistants	156.80	Female
Clothing cutters, milliners, furriers	157.80	Female
Launderers, dry cleaners, pressers	158.00	Female
Cleaners, domestics	161.50	Female

In 1964 women athletes were not allowed to race at any distance over 800 metres because it was believed that they were not strong enough to run further at speed without suffering injury. In 1993 they competed at all distances, up to and beyond the marathon.

◄ **SOURCE 9**
Ann Packer wins the 800 metres Olympic gold medal in 1964

► **SOURCE 10**
Liz McColgan wins the 10,000 metres World Championship gold medal in 1993

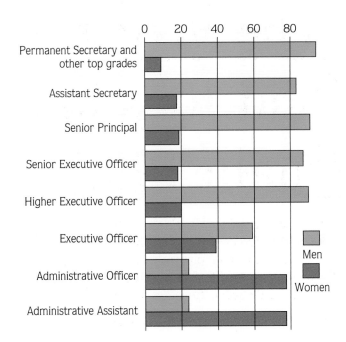

▲**SOURCE 11** This graph shows the percentage of men and women at different grades in the Civil Service in 1991. The highest grades and better-paid jobs are at the top

Equal abilities, equal rights?

A Women have the same abilities as men, but they have not had the same opportunities to use them. Where they do have the same opportunities as men, they perform just as well as men.

B Women have different abilities from of men. Women are good at caring and loving, whereas men are good at being competitive and aggressive. Society needs both, so it needs to maintain the distinction between men's and women's social roles.

C Women have different abilities from men, but society does not value women's abilities. Society needs to change, so that women's qualities are valued as well as men's.

▲**SOURCE 12** A number of different viewpoints on women's position in society

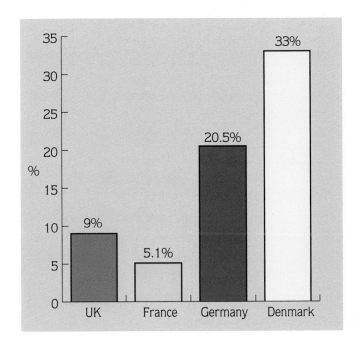

▲**SOURCE 13** The percentage of women Members of Parliament in some European countries in 1990

2. In 1975 the Sex Discrimination Act made it illegal to discriminate against women in education, jobs, housing or services. How do you think the government might justify the situation described by Sources 11 and 13?

Activity

1. Take a class vote. Which of the statements in Source 12 do you most agree with?
2. Which might a campaigner for women's rights agree with?
3. Who might agree with the other statements?
Now work in pairs to prepare for a class debate. Take one statement you agree with and one you disagree with. Find evidence in this book to support or attack each viewpoint.

Childbirth: a duty or a pleasure?

The perils of childbirth

From the Middle Ages to the present day women's lives have been greatly affected by the fact that it is they who give birth to children and they who usually look after them.

For virtually the whole of the period we have been looking at childbirth was dangerous as well as painful. It was dangerous for the baby. Even in rich families many babies died. King Henry VIII could afford the best medical care, yet seven of his first wife's eight babies died. As you saw on page 21, it was seen as part of God's punishment of Eve that childbirth should be painful.

Childbirth was also dangerous for the mother. It was the main cause of death amongst women of childbearing age until well into the twentieth century. All the women that we have looked at in this book, from Alice Coleman in medieval Northamptonshire to Josephine Butler in nineteenth-century Oxford, would have lived with this knowledge.

Without adequate contraception women sometimes got pregnant when they did not want to. But even if a woman wanted a baby, the news that she was pregnant would be accompanied by anxiety as well as joy, since the end result could be the death of the baby, the mother or both.

Sources 1–5 describe various experiences of childbirth from the Middle Ages to the nineteenth century.

> **SOURCE 1** Extracts from the seventeenth-century diary of Alice Thornton. In 1652 she was twenty-seven years old
>
> **6 August 1652** *About seven weeks after I married it pleased God to give me the blessing of conception. The first quarter I was exceeding sick in breeding, after which I was strong and healthy, I bless God. Mr Thornton had a desire I should visit his friends. I passed down on foot a very high wall . . . Each step did very much strain me . . . This killed my sweet infant in my womb . . . who lived not so long as we could get a minister to baptise it . . . After the miscarriage I fell into a most terrible shaking fever . . . The hair on my head came off, my nails on my fingers and toes came off, my teeth did shake, and ready to come out and grew black . . .*
>
> *Alice Thornton, my second child, was born at Hipswell near Richmond in Yorkshire the 3rd day of January, 1654.*
>
> *Elizabeth Thornton, my third child, was born at Hipswell the 14th of February, 1655. [This child died 5 September 1656.]*
>
> *Katherine Thornton, my fourth child, was born at Hipswell . . . the 12th of June, 1656.*
>
> *On the delivery of my first son and fifth child at Hipswell the 10th of December, 1657 . . . the child stayed in the birth, and came crosswise with his feet first, and in this condition continued till Thursday morning . . . at which I was upon the rack in bearing my child with such exquisite torments, as if each limb were divided from the other . . . but the child was almost strangled in the birth, only living about half an hour, so died before we could get a minister to baptise him . . .*
>
> **17 April 1660** *It was the pleasure of God . . . to bring forth my sixth child . . . a very goodly son . . . after a hard labour and hazardous. [The child died two weeks later.]*
>
> **19 September 1662** *I was delivered of Robert Thornton . . . it pleased the great God to lay upon me, his weak handmaid, an exceeding great weakness, beginning, a little after my child was born, by a most violent and terrible flow of blood, with such excessive floods all that night that my dear husband, and children and friends had taken their last farewell.*
>
> **23 September 1665** *[She was pregnant once more.] I being terrified with my last extremity, could have little hopes to be preserved this time . . . if my strength were not in the Almighty . . . It pleased the Lord to make me happy with a goodly strong child, a daughter, after an exceeding sharp and perilous time. [The child died on 24 January.]*
>
> *Christopher Thornton, my ninth child, was born on Monday, the 11th of November 1667. It pleased his Saviour to deliver him out of this miserable world on the 1st of December, 1667.*

---

1. Read Source 1. How many of Alice Thornton's babies lived to the age of one?
2. How many years of her life were taken up with childbearing?

▶ **SOURCE 2** Sir Thomas Aston at the deathbed of his wife, who died in childbirth, painted by John Souch in 1635

SOURCE 3 A story from the *Carmarthen Journal*, 19 July 1867. Mary Rees was an unmarried servant in the house of a businessman in Aberystwyth. She was on trial for the murder of her baby

"When Mary Rees became pregnant she didn't tell her employer, knowing that otherwise she would lose her job. So when the baby was born she gave birth in the night, unaided, silently enduring the pains of childbirth in the room that she shared with another servant.

In the morning the other girl became suspicious when she saw Mary wiping spots of blood from the floor, and when she carried the slop bucket to the outside toilet, covered by her apron. The baby's body was found later that morning in the toilet, with marks around its neck to show that it had been strangled.

Mary was sentenced to four months in prison with hard labour."

SOURCE 4 A nineteenth-century tombstone in Yorkshire

"In memory of
John Sixsmith.
Died June 14th 1896, aged 78 years.
Also Ellen his wife.
Died August 21st 1886, aged 68 years.
Also their children,

	Born	Died
Hannah	1838	1838
Joseph	1839	1839
Daniel	1840	1840
Margaret	1841	1844
Margaret	1846	1852
William	1850	1851
Alice	1852	1852
Ann	1853	1861
Elizabeth	1853	1862
Ellen	1855	1861
John Thomas	1858	1861

Weep not for us your children dear,
Nor wish us back again;
For we have earned a heavenly home,
No more to suffer pain."

▲**SOURCE 5** A birth by Caesarian section, painted in the Middle Ages. This dangerous and often fatal operation was only carried out in extreme cases, when the mother was likely to die anyway

3. What impression of childbirth do Sources 1–5 give you?
4. Do you think it is an accurate impression?
5. Make a list of all the problems associated with childbirth through the ages that you can find in Sources 1–5.

CHILDBIRTH: A DUTY OR A PLEASURE?

Midwives

In the Middle Ages most women were helped to give birth by other women. It was unusual for men – even the husband – to be present. Even operations such as Caesarian sections were performed by women (see Source 5). Usually, the midwife would be a local woman who had helped at many other births. Often, she was the wise-woman from the village, who used herbal remedies and cures to limit pain and to fight infections after the birth.

1. Source 6 was painted 200 years after Source 3. What had changed?

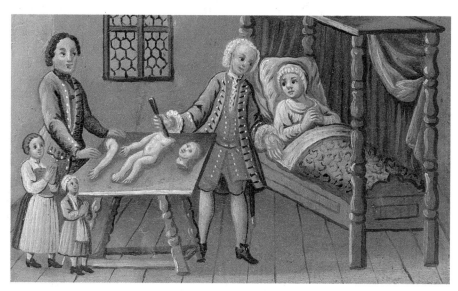

▲**SOURCE 6** An engraving made in the 1700s showing the tragic results of forceps delivery by a doctor

The doctors take over

In the seventeenth century men began to take over medical care. Medicine was becoming more scientific, and more training was needed to understand all the new discoveries about the body that were being made. Since only men could go to the universities where medicine was taught, only men could be doctors.

Doctors began to have a much greater role in childbirth – particularly in wealthy households. Midwives would still help, but the doctor was now in charge. Some male doctors were suspicious of midwives. They thought their techniques were unscientific and based on superstition. Indeed, some midwives were accused of being witches in the sixteenth and seventeenth centuries. In some places laws were passed to stop women 'meddling in surgery'.

Doctors tried out new techniques for assisting women to give birth. One of the problems that many women had was that the position or size of the baby made it difficult to push it out. Forceps, which fitted around the head of the baby, were developed in the seventeenth century (see Source 7). They could be used to free the baby's head if it was stuck. However, if they were used carelessly, forceps often damaged the baby's head and injured the mother. Only doctors were allowed to use forceps. Gradually, rich women began to prefer a male doctor to help them in childbirth, instead of a local midwife.

Despite these developments, childbirth remained a dangerous experience in the nineteenth century. One in five mothers died in childbirth, and one in six births resulted in the death of the baby.

▼**SOURCE 7** An engraving made in 1786 showing the use of forceps to free a baby's head

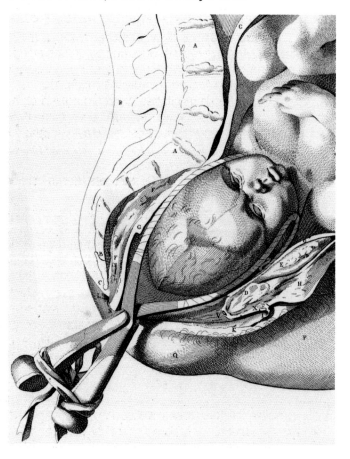

SOURCE 8 Books about pregnancy and childbirth now encourage women to feel positive about the experience of pregnancy and to see their 'roundness as something that is ripening and creating'

However, there were some important developments. The first anaesthetics were developed in the 1840s, and Queen Victoria was given chloroform as a painkiller during the birth of her eighth child in 1853. Florence Nightingale, who had helped transform standards of hygiene in nursing, turned her attention to training midwives. She focused on the need for cleanliness and hygiene in childbirth. However, she never had as much success in this area as she did in hospitals. Even in the late 1800s most poor mothers would still give birth attended by an untrained midwife.

In the second half of the twentieth century developments in medical care and pain relief have finally transformed childbirth.

■ New methods of pain relief such as epidurals (a type of anaesthetic) mean that, if she so desires, the mother can feel no pain at all.

■ Caesarians can be performed as safely as any other operations.

■ Small, premature or sick babies can be kept alive and cared for by modern, high-tech methods.

■ Nowadays only one in 60,000 mothers dies in childbirth and only one in 200 births results in the death of the baby.

With most of the dangers a thing of the past, childbirth has now begun to be treated as a great and fulfilling emotional experience, something to be celebrated and enjoyed. In fact, some women have turned their backs on the very medical advances that have made this change possible. They say that as doctors have become more involved in childbirth, it has been treated as a medical problem, with the mother seen as a sick patient.

Many women now prefer to have their babies at home or in a hospital environment that feels less medical. For example, some have babies in birthing pools. Most births are attended by a midwife and often by the father of the baby. The doctors only become involved if complications develop with the birth.

---

1. Look back at the problems associated with childbirth on page 79.
2. Explain whether and how each of these problems has been overcome.

Contraception

Until the nineteenth century contraception was unreliable and illegal. Anyone giving advice to women on how to use contraception could be imprisoned.

Over the last 100 years this situation has been transformed for many people.

■ In 1860 over half of the families in England and Wales had five or more children. Working-class mothers spent, on average, fifteen years either pregnant or looking after a child under one year old.

■ In 1877 Charles Bradlaugh and Annie Besant were taken to court for publishing a book giving information about birth control.

■ In 1921 Marie Stopes opened a family planning clinic in London giving out free advice and cheap contraceptives.

■ By 1930 the Family Planning Association had been formed. National birth control clinics were started around the country. Every local authority was obliged to have one by 1967.

■ By the 1950s one in ten women did not have children at all.

■ In the 1960s the contraceptive pill was introduced. This was the most reliable means of contraception yet developed and it was also convenient and entirely under the control of the woman.

■ In 1967 abortion became legal in Britain. Now a woman could end a pregnancy if she really wanted or needed to. There are thousands of abortions each year, although there is also a strong anti-abortion movement.

■ In 1991 the average British family had less than two children. One woman in five now does not have children at all.

■ In 1994 the Roman Catholic Church, which has millions of followers in Britain, confirmed that it still bans its members from using contraception.

Is childcare getting harder?

THROUGHOUT this book you have seen how women have taken responsibility for childcare. Looking after children has dominated many women's lives. It has prevented them having well-paid jobs and so has made them dependent on their husbands' income. They have had to juggle the demands of childcare with the demands of housework, cooking and helping their husband in his work. In the nineteenth century Parliament passed laws forbidding women from taking certain jobs that were thought to prevent them looking after their children properly.

The burden that childcare places on women has always varied according to whether they are rich or poor. Throughout the period you have studied the rich had servants, wet-nurses, nannies and boarding-schools to take the strain. The poor, on the other hand, had to find ways of coping by themselves. Poor people married at a later age than the rich. Until the nineteenth century poor women had fewer children than rich women. Older relatives and friends would help out. Even young children were quickly taught to earn their keep by helping to earn money or doing the housework.

In the Middle Ages babies were tightly wrapped, or 'swaddled', in bands of cloth. The main idea of swaddling was to make the limbs grow straight, but it also restricted movement. This meant that the child could be left unattended while the mother got on with her work. It has even been suggested that the swaddled babies were sometimes hung up on hooks to keep them out of harm's way.

The Fashionable Mamma, — or — The Convenience of Modern Dress

▲SOURCE 1 A cartoon by James Gilray, showing a servant bringing a baby for its feed

◄SOURCE 2 This medieval picture shows a swaddled baby

1. Look at Sources 1 and 2. How are the problems faced by the rich mother and the poor mother similar, and how are they different?
2. Can you find other sources in this book that show how
a) rich women
b) poor women
coped with childcare?

82

In the twentieth century a number of inventions have been designed to help solve some of the problems of childcare, as you can see in Source 3.

However, taking some of the danger and drudgery out of the job has not necessarily meant that looking after children takes less time. In the early twentieth century the hard-pressed mother was encouraged to leave a young baby in a pram outside in the fresh air for hours on end while she got on with her housework. The modern mother, although freed of some of those chores, still has to manage the housework, often without the help of her husband or other people in the family, but is also expected to stimulate and educate the child, paying attention to its emotional as well as its physical needs.

> **3.** Explain how each of the features shown in Source 3 can make childcare easier.

SOURCE 3 Some of the modern childcare-aids available to parents

SOURCE 4 Written by Penelope Leach in her book *Baby and Child* in 1977

66 *It is easy to get so involved in your baby's daily care that you find yourself treating her as if she were a very precious kind of object rather than a developing person; a new human being . . . Don't let night feeds and wet nappies take up so much of your attention that you miss the fascinating changes which are taking place in her: the signs of her beginning to grow up.*

All the vital developments . . . are waiting inside your baby. She has a built-in drive to practise every aspect of being human, from making sounds, using her hands or rolling over, to eating real food or roaring with laughter. But each aspect is also in your hands. You can help her develop and learn or you can hinder her by holding yourself aloof. You can keep her happy and busy and learning fast or you can keep her discontented, bored and not learning as fast as she could. 99

IS CHILDCARE GETTING HARDER?

The perfect carer?

Sources 5–8 were all published in the 1990s. They give contrasting views of what it is like to look after children in Britain today.

▼**SOURCE 5** A cartoon by Ros Asquith which was published in a 1990 book, *Baby*

'All this waffle about women's oppression — life just isn't like that anymore'

◄ **SOURCE 6**
A single parent living in bed and breakfast accommodation in Suffolk in the 1990s

Folding High/Low Chairs

This type also converts easily from highchair to lowchair but has the added advantage of being a folding chair as well.

TOMY ADJUST-A-HEIGHT £70
Practical highchair which converts easily to lowchair but also has six alternative height settings in between. Extra large tray for ease at mealtimes. Folds in any position. Ref 2967

BOOSTER CUSHION
Ref 4617   **£11.99**
Not illustrated.

PLAY HEIGHT

Activity

1. Work in groups of three.
   Imagine you are the editorial board of a national childcare magazine. You have the four pictures in Sources 5–8. Which of them are you going to use in your magazine? You can use all or just some of them.
   Decide which you will use and how you will use them. Write a paragraph to go with each picture to explain to your readers what it tells you about childcare today.
2. Choose one picture from earlier in this book which shows that childcare has changed, and one to show that it has stayed the same. Write a paragraph to explain your choice of pictures.

---

1. Look at Sources 5–8. Do they agree about:
   a) who is responsible for childcare in Britain today
   b) what it is like to look after children today?
2. What reasons can you think of to explain the differences between these sources?

Has domestic technology made women's lives easier?

SINCE THE Middle Ages, women have been largely responsible for housework. They may have been helped by their children or by other family members, but still they have been expected to do most of the cooking, washing, cleaning and childcare. The evidence on the next three pages shows how housework has changed since the Middle Ages.

1. **Washing clothes** Peasants did not wash their clothes very often. They did not have soap. And they did not have irons.
2. **Water** was collected collected from a nearby stream or well.
3. **Cooking** A large pot over an open fire was ideal for cooking soup or peas and beans which were the main diet of poor people.
4. **Breadmaking** Bread was another important food. Women made bread dough at home. They marked the dough, then took it to a shared village oven for baking.
5. **Washing up** People ate with their fingers so there was not much washing up.
6. **Cleaning** Animals sometimes shared the room with the family. The straw covering the floor would be changed regularly.
7. Bacon wrapped in a cloth.
8. Chicken cooking in an earthenware jar.
9. Peas and beans in a linen cloth suspended in the water. A pudding could be cooked in a similar way.
10. When the cooking was finished the hot water in the pot could be used for washing.

Activity

Work in groups of three.
1. Choose either 1300, 1850 or 1990 and use pictures and captions to show how water was obtained, food cooked, clothes washed and houses cleaned in that year.
2. Compare your accounts with those of the other two in the group. Look for two examples of great change between periods and two examples of continuity.

SOURCE 1 1300

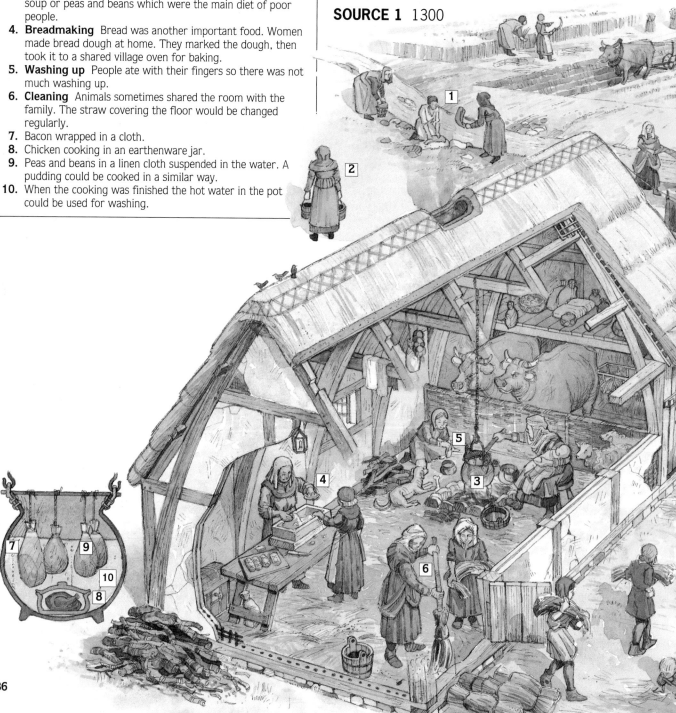

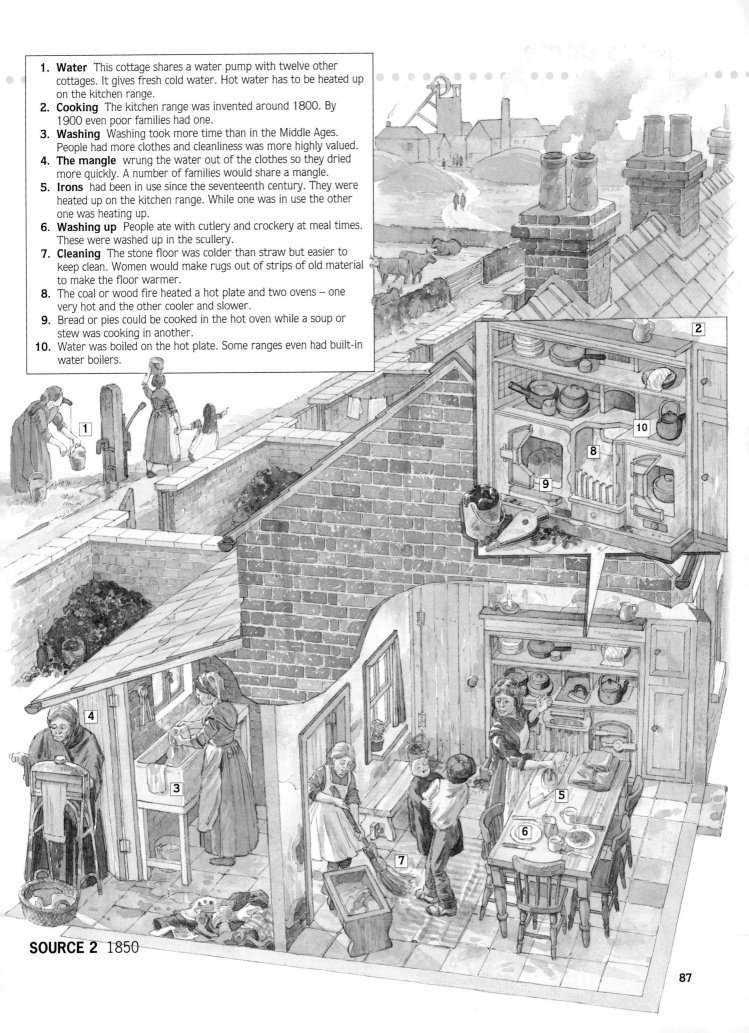

1. **Water** This cottage shares a water pump with twelve other cottages. It gives fresh cold water. Hot water has to be heated up on the kitchen range.
2. **Cooking** The kitchen range was invented around 1800. By 1900 even poor families had one.
3. **Washing** Washing took more time than in the Middle Ages. People had more clothes and cleanliness was more highly valued.
4. **The mangle** wrung the water out of the clothes so they dried more quickly. A number of families would share a mangle.
5. **Irons** had been in use since the seventeenth century. They were heated up on the kitchen range. While one was in use the other one was heating up.
6. **Washing up** People ate with cutlery and crockery at meal times. These were washed up in the scullery.
7. **Cleaning** The stone floor was colder than straw but easier to keep clean. Women would make rugs out of strips of old material to make the floor warmer.
8. The coal or wood fire heated a hot plate and two ovens – one very hot and the other cooler and slower.
9. Bread or pies could be cooked in the hot oven while a soup or stew was cooking in another.
10. Water was boiled on the hot plate. Some ranges even had built-in water boilers.

SOURCE 2 1850

HAS DOMESTIC TECHNOLOGY MADE WOMEN'S LIVES EASIER?

Has life become easier for women?

From the late eighteenth century onwards there was a huge explosion in the number of household gadgets available.

To start with, only the rich could afford them but, as they had servants to do the work anyway, they often did not bother to buy such machines. Gradually, the prices of household appliances came down to the point where many poorer families could also afford them. Today, most houses will have machines to help in almost all domestic chores.

It is usually assumed that these inventions made life easier for women because they reduced the amount of time spent on housework. While it is undoubtedly true that household gadgets do reduce the time needed to do housework, some historians have argued that improvements in domestic technology may have had a different consequence: they raised people's expectations of women.

1. **Water** Virtually all homes in Britain have hot and cold running water on tap.
2. **Cooking** Virtually all houses have a cooker. Some also have a microwave oven. This cooks pre-prepared meals in minutes.
3. **Bread** Most people buy bread from a shop instead of making it themselves.
4. **Washing** Many houses have washing machines. Other families take their washing to a Launderette. Some houses have dishwashers.
5. **Cleaning** Vacuum cleaners were invented early in the twentieth century. Most households now own one.

SOURCE 3 1990

SOURCE 4

A *Superwoman's Day*, a cartoon drawn by Posy Simmonds in 1983. A book called *Superwoman*, suggesting that it was possible for a woman to be successful in all the different and conflicting areas of her life, had recently become a bestseller

For example, as machines used for cleaning improved, people began to expect higher standards of cleanliness. Medieval peasants would not have expected a clean set of clothes each day – washing was a less important domestic task than fetching water. Nowadays, on the other hand, because cleanliness is possible, it has become highly valued, and a woman can spend much more of her time on washing than she needs to.

Similarly, as families acquire more possessions, there are more things to keep clean. Compare the bare interior of the cottage on page 86 with your own living room. Which would be the easiest to keep clean?

Now that domestic tasks are performed more quickly and efficiently by machines, women are expected to do a whole new range of domestic tasks.

Many recent writers have suggested that women are now expected to keep their families better-clothed, better-housed, better-fed and generally happier than in previous ages, as well as earning extra money, keeping the family accounts, and so on.

SOURCE 5 Written by Ruth Cowan in 1970

6 *Increased expectations have placed new demands on a woman's time by increasing the number of functions that she is expected to perform – from nutritionist, to shopper, to electrical repairwoman, to semi-professional psychiatrist.* 9

1. Look at Source 4. Make a list of the roles the cartoonist suggests a woman needs to play.
2. Read Source 5. Add to your list the roles the writer suggests.
3. From your work on this book or from your own knowledge, can you add any more to the list?
4. Choose three roles from your list and add three frames to Posy Simmonds' cartoon as part of Superwoman's day. You can get a sheet from your teacher to help you.

1. Look back over pages 86–88 and find one invention that you think improved life for most women, and one example of an invention that did not. Explain your choice.
2. Do you think that improved domestic technology has made women's lives easier? Write a paragraph to explain your answer.

Images of women through the ages

THROUGH most of history both men and women have believed that a woman should try to look beautiful. But what people think is beautiful or 'ideal' has changed a lot over time. Can you match the descriptions of the ideal woman on page 91 with Sources 1–5?

▶ SOURCE 1

▲SOURCE 2

◀ SOURCE 3

INTIMITÉ

▲SOURCE 4

▼SOURCE 5

Descriptions

A Prehistoric
The ideal prehistoric female was hugely fat. Such a woman would have had reserves of energy to enable her to live through periods of food shortage while pregnant or breast-feeding a baby.

B Medieval
In the Middle Ages the ideal woman among the upper classes would have had fair skin and a thin waist. The ideal physical qualities for a working peasant woman would have been health, strength and stamina.

C Sixteenth to eighteenth centuries
From the sixteenth to the eighteenth centuries plumpness became fashionable once more. Female fashions emphasised large busts and hips. Skirts and petticoats had large hoops sewn into them to make them full. This would contrast with the starved appearance of many poorer people.

D Nineteenth century
In the ninteenth century the ideal woman, 'the angel in the house', was delicate, almost weak and sickly. After the 1820s fashions emphasised the woman's delicate and slender waist. Many women wore uncomfortable corsets to compress their waists.

E The 1920s
In the 1920s there was a strong reaction to the style and image of the nineteenth century. Narrow waists went out of fashion. Women were still expected to be thin, but not pale or sickly. Women's clothes become more daring and hairstyles much simpler.

1. Use the descriptions to match Sources 1–5 to the correct period. Explain your choice.
2. Why do you think the image of an ideal women has changed over time?
3. Many people would say that these images of women are stereotypes – they only show an ideal – and that real women of the period did not look like this. How would you set about finding out whether or not this was true?
4. Write your own description of what the image of the 'ideal' woman is today.
5. Which of the other descriptions is it most similar to, and which is it most different from?
6. Has the image of the ideal man changed and developed over time, too?

Alternative images of women

Even stereotypes are powerful images. Many people feel that today's images of ideal female beauty in advertisements or films are so powerful that they are damaging. People argue that they form an impossible ideal, which ordinary women try to live up to with dangerous results. For example, when the ideal woman is portrayed as thin, many women try dangerous diets in order to look thin, too.

In response to this worry, some female artists and photographers have attempted to show newer and truer images of women. They show them as ordinary people living active lives.

▲SOURCE 6

Activity

Work in groups to make a display which compares 'ideal' images with 'real' images.

Collect together pictures of women in modern situations. You could get them from recent newspapers and magazines. You could also use family snaps or take photos around your school or community.

On your display write an explanation of how the 'ideal' image is similar to or different from the 'real' image.

◀ SOURCE 7   ▲SOURCE 8

Acknowledgements

p.2 *top left* Copyright Bibliothèque royale Albert 1er, Bruxelles; *top right* Empics/Popperfoto; *bottom left* By permission of the National Museum of Labour History; *bottom right* Mary Evans/Fawcett Library. **p.3** *top left* The Bodleian Library, Oxford; *top right* Bridgeman Art Library, London; *centre* © Ros Asquith, reproduced by kind permission; *bottom* Forschungs- und Landesbibliothek, Gotha (Chart. A 689, f.156). **p.5** Glasgow Museums: The Burrell Collection. **p.6** © Marsaili Cameron. **p.7** *top left* By permission of The British Library (MS Harl. 1892, f.27v); *top right* By permission of The British Library (MS Sloane, 3983, f.5); *centre right* The Bodleian Library, Oxford (MS Bodl. 764, f.41v); *bottom left* Peter Dunn/English Heritage. **p.8** *top* By permission of The British Library (MS Harl 2838, f.37); *bottom* Bayerische Staatsbibliothek (MS cod. gall. 16, f.20v). **p.9** *top left* The Walters Art Gallery, Baltimore (MS W. 249, f.119); *top right* © Rijksmuseum-Stichting Amsterdam; *centre left* Bibliothèque Nationale, Paris/Bridgeman Art Library; *centre* Österreichische Nationalbibliothek, Vienna (COD.s.nov. 2644, f.82v); *centre right* National Gallery of Victoria, Melbourne, Australia, Felton Bequest, 1922 (d'Aspremont Hours: The Offices of the Virgin, f.4v); *bottom* The Walters Art Gallery, Baltimore (MS W. 88, ff.14v-15). **p.10** By permission of The British Library (MS Egerton 1894, f.9v). **p.12** The Bodleian Library, Oxford (MS Douce 6, f.97v). **p.13** *top left* The Pierpont Morgan Library/Art Resource, N.Y. (MS 917, f.149); *bottom left* Fitzwilliam Museum, Cambridge (MS 159); *bottom right* The Bodleian Library, Oxford (MS Douce 6, f.22). **p.14** By permission of The British Library (MS Harl 4380, f.6). **p.16** *top left* The Bodleian Library, Oxford (MS Douce 195, f.118); *top right* By permission of The British Library (MS Roy. 15 D I, f.18); *bottom* Forschungs- und Landesbibliothek, Gotha (Chart. A 689, f.156). **p.17** *top right* Österreichische Nationalbibliothek, Vienna (COD. 93, f.102). **p.18** *centre* Bayerische Staatsbibliothek (from Johann Schwartzenberg, Memorial der Tugend, Augsburg 1535); *bottom* The Pierpont Morgan Library/Art Resource N.Y. (MS 1001, f.48). **p.21** By permission of The British Library (MS Add. 10546, f.5v). **p.22** The Pierpont Morgan Library/Art Resource, N.Y. (MS 917, f.151). **p.23** Giraudon/Bridgeman Art Library, London. **p.24** By permission of The British Library (MS Cott. Dom. A. XVII, f.177v). **p.25** *top left* Collections du Musée de l'Assistance Publique-Hôpitaux de Paris; *top right* Archivi Alinari. **p.27** *left* Tate Gallery, London; *right* By permission of The British Library (G13664). **p.29** *top* Roy Miles Gallery/Bridgeman Art Library, London; *centre* Reproduction by courtesy of The Marquess of Salisbury (Photo: The Fotomas Index); *bottom* E.T. Archive. **p.30** Scottish National Portrait Gallery. **p.31** *left* Scottish National Portrait Gallery; *right* Woburn Abbey, Bedfordshire/Bridgeman Art Library, London. **p.32** Mary Evans Picture Library. **p.33** © BBC. **p.35** *top right and bottom left* Fortean Picture Library; *bottom right* Hulton Deutsch Collection. **p.38** *top left* Fortean Picture Library; *top right* Hulton Deutsch Collection; *bottom* The Huntingdon Library, San Marino, California. **p.39** The Archbishop of Canterbury and the Trustees of Lambeth Palace Library. **p.40** By permission of The British Library (E1150 (5)). **p.41** By permission of The British Library (E618 (8)). **p.42** *top and bottom* Mary Evans Picture Library. **p.43** The Mansell Collection. **p.44** *top* © Manchester City Art Galleries; *bottom* Mary Evans Picture Library. **p.45** By permission of the National Museum of Labour History. **p.47** Hulton Deutsch Collection. **p.48** Hulton Deutsch Collection. **p.49** *top* and *bottom* Hulton Deutsch Collection; **p.50** *top* Hulton Deutsch Collection; *centre and bottom left* Mary Evans Picture Library; *bottom right* Rural History. Centre, University of Reading. **p.51** Mary Evans Picture Library. **p.52** Tate Gallery, London. **p.55** *left* Hulton Deutsch Collection; *right* Royal Academy of Arts, London. **p.56** Hulton Deutsch Collection. **p.59** Mary Evans/Fawcett Library. **p.60** Mary Evans Picture Library. **p.62** *top left* Hulton Deutsch Collection; *bottom* Mary Evans/Fawcett Library. **p.63** *left and right* Hulton Deutsch Collection. **p.64** *top and centre* Mary Evans Picture Library; *bottom* Mary Evans/Fawcett Library. **p.66** Imperial War Museum (Q28391). **p.67** *top* Hulton Deutsch Collection; *bottom* Imperial War Museum (Q31239). **p.68** Mary Evans/Fawcett Library. **p.69** John Frost Historical Newspapers. **p.71** *top* Hulton Deutsch Collection; *bottom left and right* Mary Evans Picture Library. **p.72** Hulton Deutsch Collection. **p.75** *top left* Empics/Popperfoto; *bottom right* Advertisement reproduced courtesy of Candy Domestic Appliances and illustration by Frances Lloyd/Courtesy of House Beautiful magazine. **p.76** *top* Reproduced courtesy of the Low Pay Unit; *bottom left* Allsport UK; *bottom right* Gray Mortimore/Allsport UK. **p.79** *top* © Manchester City Art Galleries; *bottom* By permission of The British Library (MS Roy. 16. G. VII, f.219). **p.80** *top* Bayerisches National Museum, Munich; *bottom* By permission of The British Library (1831b19). **p.81** © Sally and Richard Greenhill. **p.82** *top* © British Museum; *bottom* By permission of The British Library (MS Add. 38122, f.73v). **p.83** John Townson/Creation. **p.84** *top* © Ros Asquith, reproduced by kind permission; *bottom* © Jacky Chapman/Format. **p.85** *top* © Michael Heath, reproduced by kind permission; *bottom* Reproduced courtesy of Early Learning Centre. **p.89** Reprinted by permission of the Peters Fraser and Dunlop Group Ltd. **p.90** *top left* Museum der bildenden Künste Leipzig; *top right* Ali Meyer/Bridgeman Art Library, London; *bottom* Mansell Collection. **p.91** *top* and *bottom* Mary Evans Picture Library. **p.92** *top and bottom right* © Ulrike Preuss/Format; *bottom left* © Jacky Chapman/Format.

Every effort has been made to trace all the copyright holders, but if any have been inadvertently overlooked, the publishers will be pleased to make the necessary arrangement at the first opportunity.

Index